The Portable

PROCRASTINATOR

DOODLE PAD

Get Busy Wasting Time

Running Press
Philadelphia • London

© 2007 by Production Line Limited

First published in the United States in 2007 by Running Press Book Publishers

All rights reserved under the Pan-American and International Copyright Conventions

'The Portable Procrastinator' and 'The Procrastinator' are trademarks of Production Line Limited

Production Line are designers and manufacturers of good ideas.

Production Line Limited, The Village Studio, Heol y Coed, Rhiwbina, Cardiff, United Kingdom, CF14 6HP

www.theprocrastinator.co.uk

Printed in Canada

9 8 7 6 5 4 3 2 1

Digit on the right indicates the number of this printing

ISBN-13: 978-0-7624-2881-6

ISBN-10: 0-7624-2881-3

This book may be ordered by mail from the publisher. Please include $2.50 for postage and handling.

But try your bookstore first!

Running Press Book Publishers
2300 Chestnut Street
Philadelphia, PA 19103-4371

Visit us on the web!
www.runningpress.com

The Portable Procrastinator

The Portable Procrastinator really is the essential workstation companion. Page after page crammed full of opportunities to create, comment, vote, scribble, decide, suggest, choose, design, think, report, plan, dismiss ... and generally to procrastinate.

There are no wrong answers, no solutions to find, just loads of things to do for no reason other than to amuse and to entertain.

Finish off doodles and drawings in whatever way your mind takes you. Discover its hidden depths ... surprise yourself!

Give all sorts of things a score out of ten and place lists in your order of preference. Use your imagination to create wild and elaborate images from nothing more than a title, and develop visual prompts into works of art.

Consider very important social issues and dismiss them out of hand. Select things just because you like the look of them. Nominate anyone you like, or don't like, for an award. Suggest who did what, to whom, and did they get what they deserved?

The Portable Procrastinator will get you thinking, laughing, making decisions, and will bring out the creativity in just about anybody.

So get busy wasting time - but don't get caught!

Question

Why is it that just as you are leaving for a quick lunchtime break, someone phones with a trivial but excruciatingly long, boring monologue?

Career path

Burning the midnight oil

Today's big thing

After considering all the available options, it has been decided that the monster of the day is:

Score out of 10

Paper Clip
Stapler
Rubber Band
Pen
Xerox
Binder
Punch
Thumbtack
Office Plant
Pencil

Professionals wrestling

V
V
V
V

Web of intrigue

Surprise package

Drunk voicemail

Message...................................
....
....
....

Mad texting

— — — — —
— — — — —
— — — — —

Hiring and firing

The crazy character with the cartoon tie

Hire

Fire

A bit wordy

B T

Apples and oranges

The most aggressive and the most timid

Captured on TV

I'm bored

Small beer

Work ethic

Output

Mon Tues Wed Thurs Fri Sat Sun

Brainstorming

To liven up the next team briefing

Karaoke

A loose rhino

Mood

Yesterday

Today

Tomorrow

Things not to put on your resumé

1
2
3

Killing time

Descriptive descriptions

(*n*) The realization that you've totally messed up

(*adj*) A printer which routinely shreds your work

(*v*) To sniff loudly and persistently in a meeting

Doubtful diploma

Awarded to

_____

for their

_____

_____

Signed

Running order 1-3

Running it up the flagpole

Running the company

Running with clown shoes on

Floating ideas

Shapely shapes

A very long face

Answer

The full and honest answer as to why you weren't promoted in the last round is that you are an Aquarian and Venus was rising at the time.

FREESTYLE DOODLING AREA

A long and incredibly drawn out day

A grand entrance

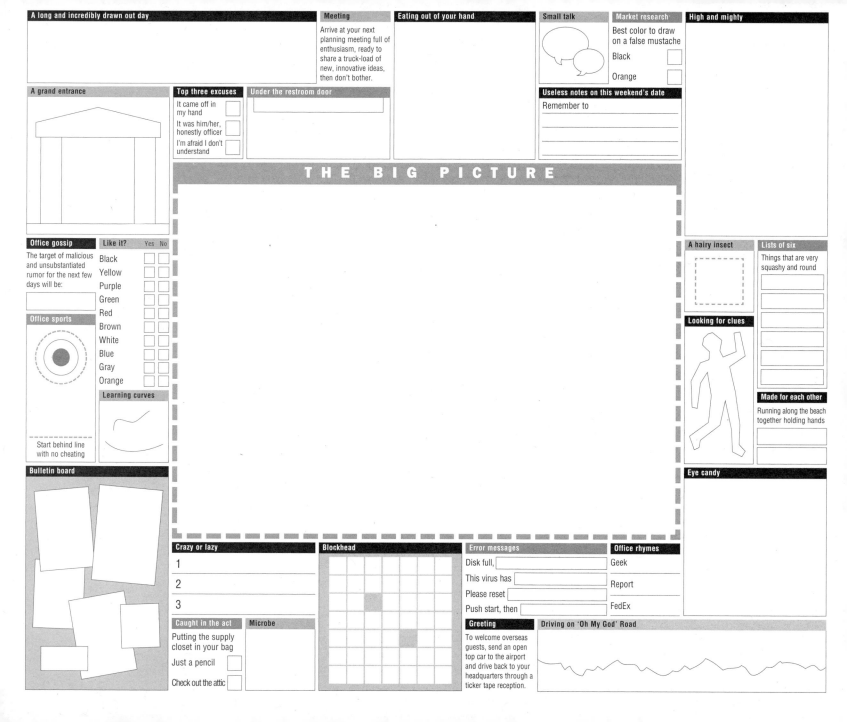

Meeting
Arrive at your next planning meeting full of enthusiasm, ready to share a truck-load of new, innovative ideas, then don't bother.

Eating out of your hand

Small talk

Market research
Best color to draw on a false mustache
Black
Orange

High and mighty

Top three excuses
It came off in my hand
It was him/her, honestly officer
I'm afraid I don't understand

Under the restroom door

Useless notes on this weekend's date
Remember to

THE BIG PICTURE

Office gossip
The target of malicious and unsubstantiated rumor for the next few days will be:

Office sports
Start behind line with no cheating

Like it?   Yes No
Black
Yellow
Purple
Green
Red
Brown
White
Blue
Gray
Orange

Learning curves

A hairy insect

Looking for clues

Lists of six
Things that are very squashy and round

Made for each other
Running along the beach together holding hands

Bulletin board

Eye candy

Crazy or lazy
1
2
3

Caught in the act
Putting the supply closet in your bag
Just a pencil
Check out the attic

Microbe

Blockhead

Error messages
Disk full,
This virus has
Please reset
Push start, then

Greeting
To welcome overseas guests, send an open top car to the airport and drive back to your headquarters through a ticker tape reception.

Office rhymes
Geek
Report
FedEx

Driving on 'Oh My God' Road

The big cheese

Shape up

Health and safety

Just got back from a workout at the gym

All fired up

Get a paramedic

Anger management course

Name

Problem

Recommended treatment

_____

_____

_____

_____

Result

Order of merit 1-3

The view in the mirror

The view up the stairwell

The view from the bridge

It just doesn't add up

159

Job descriptions

Taking something off the shelf and looking at it

Standing by a club door in a coat looking very mean

Tailgating and honking in a huge Mack truck

Shorts

Please take a seat in reception

Three idiots

_____

_____

_____

High flier

Today's diary

10:06am - 10:18am

12:32pm - 1:09pm

3:45pm - 5:00pm

Worth doing

Holding a huge carnival with samba dancers, steel band, and a massive fireworks display when you've had a reasonably pleasant day at work.

Come In!

Executive responsible for gross indecency and generally lewd behavior

MY SPACE

Fantasy bonus

A special, non-conditional bonus of

$

for nothing in particular is awarded to

The balloon goes up

Not worth doing

Working out an incredibly efficient and realistic schedule to achieve the virtually impossible and expecting your immediate superiors to cooperate.

Preferences 1-10

Wednesday am

Friday pm

Tuesday am

Monday pm

Thursday am

Friday am

Tuesday pm

Wednesday pm

Monday am

Thursday pm

Our new logo

Crapped out

Today's big thing

After considering all the available options, it has been decided that the island of the day is:

Reasons to be confident about the day

1

2

3

Dexterity test - Encircling letters

K B U P
F W E
F N A M

Clock watching

12
9 3
6

No harm done

Response time

If confronted about long overdue work

Sob uncontrollably

Run for it

Bitter rivals

Basketball teams that really hate each other

Around the table

Your move

	X	

On the agenda

Day

Date

1.

2.

3.

4.

5.

6.

Matter of opinion

The company's been infiltrated by talent

Great news ☐

Whatever! ☐

System overload

A tiny thing

Best results 1-3

Winning the Tour de France ☐

Winning in Las Vegas ☐

Winning an Academy Award ☐

Red or blue R B

Apple ☐ ☐
Movies ☐ ☐
Neck ☐ ☐
Paint ☐ ☐
Socks ☐ ☐
Cheese ☐ ☐
Ferrari ☐ ☐
Moon ☐ ☐
Cross ☐ ☐
Sky ☐ ☐

SWOT analysis

Subject - The Boss	Date
Strengths	Weaknesses
Opportunities	Threats

Clear up the mess

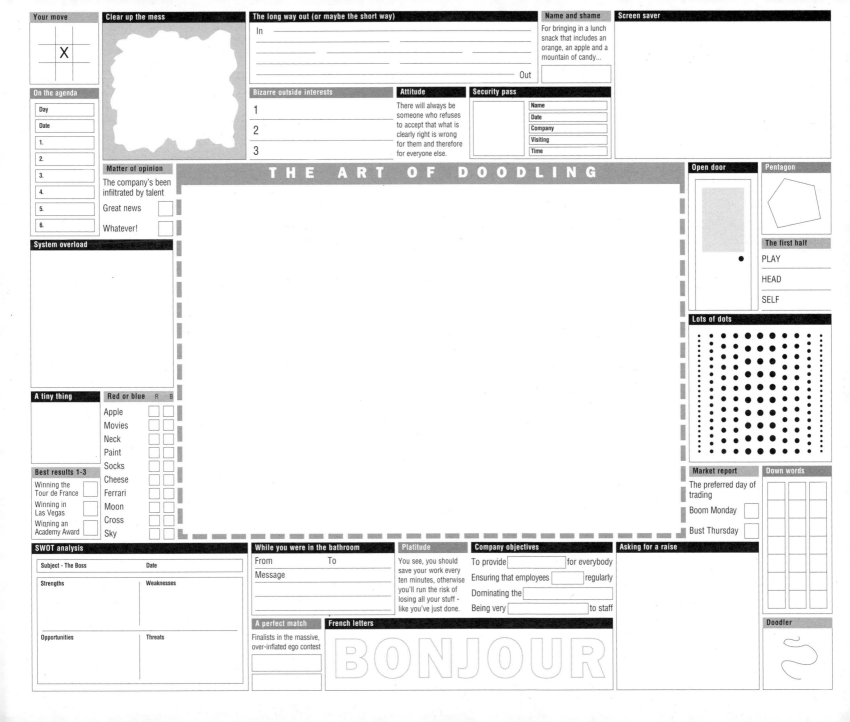

The long way out (or maybe the short way)

In _____

_____

_____

_____ Out

Bizarre outside interests

1 _____

2 _____

3 _____

Attitude

There will always be someone who refuses to accept that what is clearly right is wrong for them and therefore for everyone else.

Security pass

Name	
Date	
Company	
Visiting	
Time	

Name and shame

For bringing in a lunch snack that includes an orange, an apple and a mountain of candy...

Screen saver

THE ART OF DOODLING

While you were in the bathroom

From _____ To _____

Message _____

_____

A perfect match

Finalists in the massive, over-inflated ego contest

French letters

BONJOUR

Platitude

You see, you should save your work every ten minutes, otherwise you'll run the risk of losing all your stuff - like you've just done.

Company objectives

To provide [_____] for everybody

Ensuring that employees [_____] regularly

Dominating the [_____]

Being very [_____] to staff

Asking for a raise

Open door

•

Pentagon

The first half

PLAY

HEAD

SELF

Lots of dots

Market report

The preferred day of trading

Boom Monday [___]

Bust Thursday [___]

Down words

Doodler

Thrashing around in the dark

Triangles

Stepping stones

Reverse order 3-1
Losing billions in the crash
Losing your car keys
Losing your virginity

Eureka

New car patent

Title

Invented by

Working drawings

Signed

Mismatched
The opera diva and the wild child of rock

Vice
It started as a quick beer after work on Friday night but turned into a wild, screaming, riotous kegger where everyone ended up in the cells.

The CEO

Headhunting

Flat as a pancake

Cause and effect
Sweating profusely with an inability to speak

A desire to scream loudly out of the window

How many?
Drinks

Friends

Socks

On the horizon

Word association
Objectionable

Entertaining

Barely audible

Encouraging

Staff vote
A ban on ice cream cakes for birthdays

You bet

No way

A full and frank exchange of views - The e-mail
To

Message

From

Reply

A BLANK CANVAS

Today's big thing
After considering all the available options, it has been decided that the shellfish of the day is:

Priorities with the lottery win
1

2

3

Key proposal
'Dress as a famous historical figure' day

Lack of support

Total support

Pen-pushing
Start

Finish

The new office layout
Door

Window

Desk   Chair   Cupboard   Plant   Me

Things shown half size

Advice
You need to study hard at community college, college, grad school, business school, then finally obtain your doctorate ... and retire.

Twister

The new corporate uniform

Possessions
Windbreaker
Scotch Tape
Vaseline
Kitty Litter
Pepsi
Dumpster
Band-aids
Coke
Kleenex
Off!

All the angles

Short and sweet

Urgent status update
Name

Age

Position

Sex

Mood

Date

Plans

Shapely shapes

Places to go

1

2

3

Small arms

Classic-moment screen grab

3 words

_ _ _ _ _ _ _

_ _ _ _ _ _ _

_ _ _ _ _ _ _

A task too far

Little jobs

Selecting an appropriate paper clip, unraveling it, and attempting to make it into one long bit of wire, before losing it inside your keyboard.

Culture vulture

What happened next?

Sales

Mon Tues Wed Thurs Fri Sat Sun

New policies

To hold a yard sale every Wednesday

Agree ☐

Disagree ☐

The greasy pole

RANDOM THOUGHTS

Appointments

It is with great pleasure that we announce that the position of the next office clown goes to:

More accurate brand descriptions

The overly priced, ineffective diet plan

The car that has it all - except character

The bank that actually puts your interests first

Must have? Yes No

Muffins ☐ ☐

Popcorn ☐ ☐

Fries ☐ ☐

Goobers ☐ ☐

Donuts ☐ ☐

Oatmeal ☐ ☐

Pot roast ☐ ☐

Brownies ☐ ☐

Potato salad ☐ ☐

Steak ☐ ☐

Deep down

Main menu

Appetizer

Main Course

Dessert

Friends fighting

V

V

V

V

Window of opportunity

Time and motion

Minutes to make a coffee ☐

Hours until going home ☐

Years until retirement ☐

The big over-inflated idea

Whistle-blowing

Holding poker games in the storeroom

Acceptable ☐

Not acceptable ☐

Motivation

Yesterday

Today

Tomorrow

Where's it gone?

Dirty words

P G

Big jobs

Let's try and make the world one large global village, where we can expect ideologies of all kinds to be tolerated and exist side by side.

Twins

Difficult, obstructive, and prone to sulking

After the tone - Your mom

Message...................................

....

....

....

Little boxes

☐

☐

A man of letters

Junk mail

The memo suggesting lunchtime aerobics

In tray

Out tray

You said what?!

Technical support

Get ahead

To succeed you need to be noticed. To ensure this happens make a hat that emits an incredibly loud siren noise and has a flashing light on top.

Hung out to dry

Forgotten message

Remember to

Job search

Enter key elements that will assist your search

Results
of search

Achievements

Number of hours wasted

Opportunities turned down

Plans for the future

Life cycle

W H A T E V E R !

Lists of six

People who really should know better

Sad icon

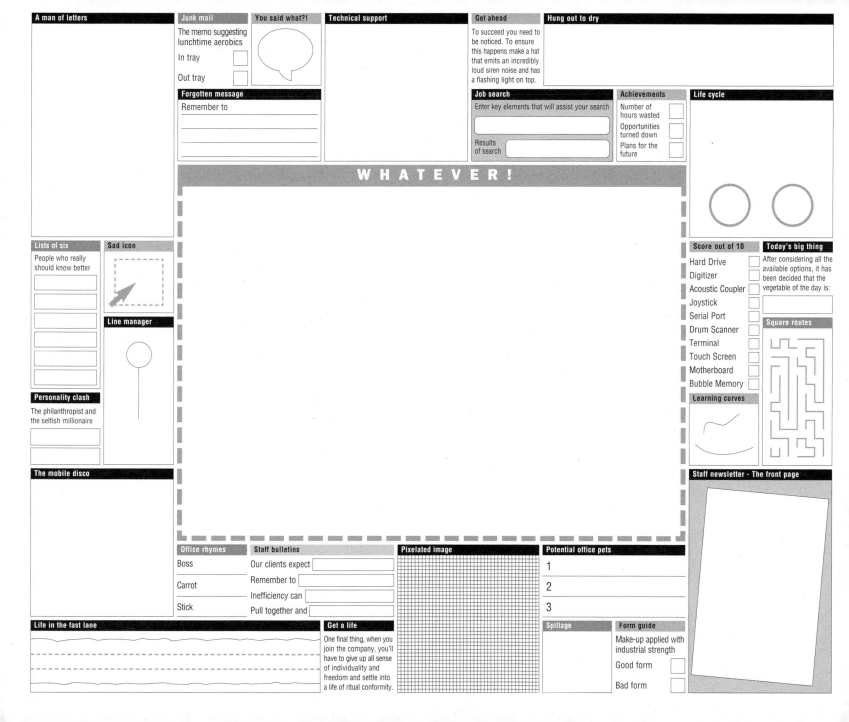

Line manager

Personality clash

The philanthropist and the selfish millionaire

Score out of 10

Hard Drive

Digitizer

Acoustic Coupler

Joystick

Serial Port

Drum Scanner

Terminal

Touch Screen

Motherboard

Bubble Memory

Today's big thing

After considering all the available options, it has been decided that the vegetable of the day is:

Square routes

Learning curves

The mobile disco

Staff newsletter - The front page

Office rhymes

Boss

Carrot

Stick

Staff bulletins

Our clients expect

Remember to

Inefficiency can

Pull together and

Pixelated image

Potential office pets

1

2

3

Life in the fast lane

Get a life

One final thing, when you join the company, you'll have to give up all sense of individuality and freedom and settle into a life of ritual conformity.

Spillage

Form guide

Make-up applied with industrial strength

Good form

Bad form

Fill the bowl, please

Professional opinion
Fine, upstanding, and dedicated pillars of society

Lowlifes that deserve to be trodden underfoot

Taking levels of total blandness to new depths

Shorthanded

Targets
Years to next promotion

Successful blind dates

Number of balls in the air

Number crunching
2 6 3

Accident report
Name

Location

Who was there

What happened (in your own words)

Shape up

Corporate gift
To welcome you into your new role

Executive toy

Executive stress

Typing pool

GET THE DOODLE BUG

High roller

Three aces

Two scribbles
Cookie

Jar

Dining
When trying to encourage the rich to support your corporate charity event perhaps a KFC and beer evening is not really the best option.

Fantasy job swap
Until further notice this permit enables

to change their job to

Whining
This is a really sick building, the air conditioning just recycles everyone's germs, the drafts play havoc with my sinuses, and I couldn't even start on the décor.

Long or short   L   S
Journey
Term
Vehicle
Vacation
Curly
Conversation
Distance
Contract
Meeting
Circuit

Post-It Note

Frustration level

Headquarters
The most corrupt company to ever get into the Fortune 500 ... allegedly

Organization chart

The weekend
A wet and wild time in a wet and wild place

Too soggy

Two tickets

Together forever
Mr. and Mrs. Squeaky Clean from Niceville

Pay and rations

Dexterity test - Copying letters
G →   B →
U →   W →

Face up

Bad habits
1
2
3

Endorsements
To promote the values of over enthusiasm to disguise very little real talent, let's hear it for:

A vicious circle

Meet the new boss, same as the old boss

Today's big thing
After considering all the available options, it has been decided that the philosophy of the day is:

Cartoon strip - The delivery boy

What's in the file?

Your move
O

Expense claim - The overnight stop
1.	$
2.	$
3.	$
4.	$
Total	$

Hardware
This new machine is great; it scans a document, applies a bullshit test based on the level of useless jargon, and then shreds anything that fails.

Favorite pies
1
2
3

Must do's
Day
Date
1.
2.
3.
4.
5.
6.

Another pentagon

Cold storage

The second half
STOP

JOB

TIME

The tree of knowledge

GIANT WHITE SPACE

Horoscope
The day will start badly and then:

steadily improve

plummet

Dressing down

Up words

Typing erors
We've put an ad out for a key employee

A surgeon

A sturgeon

Preferences 1-10
- Caffè latte
- Americano
- Skinny
- Espresso
- Cappuccino
- Double
- Mocha
- Unleaded
- Quadruple
- Macchiato

Tiny minds

A fine record
Days wearing the same shirt	
Hours without gossiping	
Minutes asleep on the desk	

Cheerleaders

Ambitions beyond reason
To write

Eating the

Jumping over

Riding a

Software
I use this screen to input all future commitments - meetings, deadlines, etc., and then upload to enable on-screen prompting. That's right, it's a diary.

While you were being told off
From   To

Message

On the back of an envelope

Doodler

It's only words
TW B OP

It'll never last
The sugar daddy and the unashamed freeloader

Facial expressions - Surprise

People to meet

1

2

3

Bored meeting

It was quite apparent that the meeting had drawn to its natural conclusion when the chair shouted out:

Acronyms explained

WOW

VCM

BBR

MOS

Homerun

Looking on the bright side

Place names - The perfect weekend break

The new recruit

A warm welcome to our new intern

Gary Cooper

Alice Cooper

Chain of command

Triangles

Twister

Good practice

Never hang out with people who tell you endless stories about themselves before saying 'That's enough about me, what do you think of me?'

The numbers game

Useless things in your head

Favorite lucky number

Your age next birthday

DRAWING ROOM

The bigger picture

Exploded view

The central nervous system

Checked   Signed

Four letters

Been there?	Yes	No
Atlanta		
Cincinnati		
Minneapolis		
Phoenix		
Tampa		
Buffalo		
Houston		
New York		
Memphis		
Los Angeles		

Short cut

Bad practice

Setting out to learn the 7 Ps of marketing, the 12 Ts of motivation, and the 34 Rs of management incompetence: all you need is the 1 F for 'Goodbye!'

Opposites attract

The most pleasant and the most objectionable

Pen-pushing

Start

Finish

Qualifications

Crucial requirements for the post

College degree

8 beers with lunch

Lowbrow

Making your pitch

One moment in time

Time		Date	
Who's in front			
Who's behind			
Who's talking			

Liquidation

How many?

Partners

Medals

Siblings

Putting it more bluntly

Encouraging people to put the coffee away

Asking for just that little bit more effort

A very, very long, good Friday

Double entry

Meeting
When making your next presentation, dispense with Powerpoint and technology and address your audience through the medium of mime.

Joined up thinking

Talk the talk

Market research
A better way of traveling to work
By donkey
By catapult

Self portrait

Top three excuses
I didn't think she'd mind
I didn't realize it was a square peg
I'm afraid that the dog ate it

Shelf life

Useless notes about work
Remember to

THE BIG PICTURE

Office gossip
You never know with this person what would happen if you pushed all the right buttons:

Office sports

Try to score from the spot

Right/Wrong   R   W
Runaway
Immoral
Angle
Normal
Turn
Mistake
Direction
Bent
Hand
Legal

Learning curves

A spiky insect

Half man

Lists of six
Things that have lots of holes in them

Made for each other
Accidentally locked in the closet together

Office paperwork

Red tape

Halfwits
1
2
3

Caught in the act
Doing absolutely nothing all day
What, me?
What's new

Plop

Square deal

Error messages
No memory
To reboot
Don't enter
Shut down

Office rhymes
Fired
Pension
Salary

Greeting
To greet clients, use a high five, some gentle pretend boxing (with dodging and weaving), and close with an over-friendly bear hug.

Bouncing along

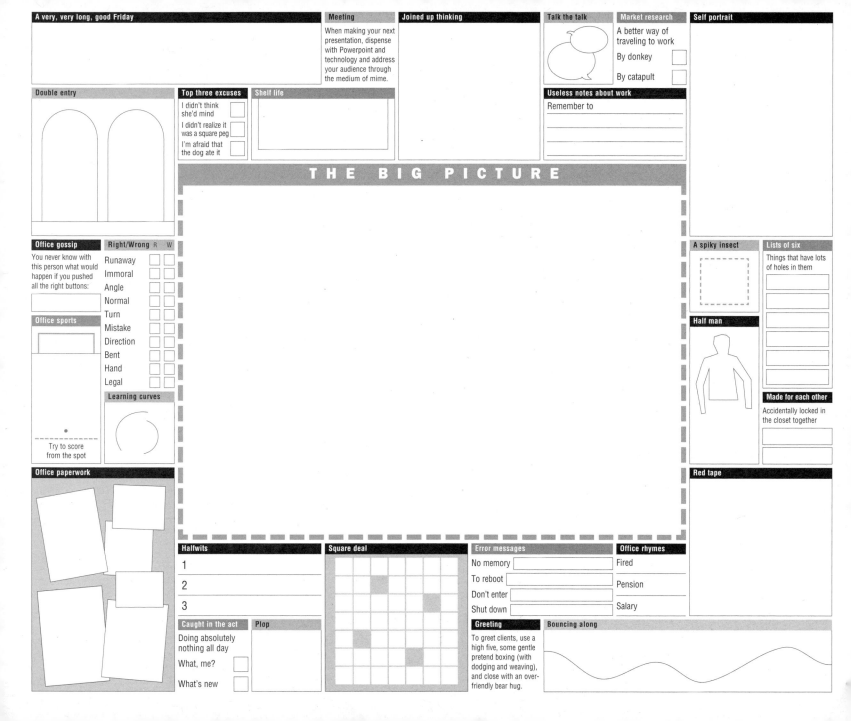

The big fish

Shape up

Sensitivity course

| Name |
| Problem |
| Objective for Participant |

Result

Health and safety

For use with the diner microwave

Novelty Apron

Welding Mask

Order of merit 1-3

The music of the 70s

The music of the 80s

The music of the 90s

Job descriptions

Filing nails, chewing, drinking coffee, and staring

Standing around in the open air pointing at things

Making life extremely difficult for everyone

Garbage

Your number's up

2 3 8

Shortcake

Three Queens

Run down

Today's diary

6:06am - 6:18am

11:10am - 12:27pm

5:23pm - 8:56pm

Worth doing

To impress your colleagues and superiors with your innovative thinking, approach the supply closet on the floor as if on commando training.

Please do come in (you look marvelous)

Director of sycophantic, fawning, and obsequious behavior

MY SPACE

Sick note

This is to confirm that the bearer has

and cannot work for at least

Rocket science

Not worth doing

Starting up a business from your own house specializing in web-based e-learning, e-business, and e-marketing and not having a computer.

Preferences 1-10

Baseball

Tennis

Football

Boxing

Golf

Nascar

Basketball

Soccer

Hockey

Track and Field

It's a sign!

Routine

Today's big thing

After considering all the available options, it has been decided that the disease of the day is:

Dexterity test - Underlining numbers

5   82   3   9

1   76   5

37   4   69   23

Blame culture

Response time

What to do if push comes to shove

Push off

Shove off

Bitter rivals

Multinationals involved in telecommunications

Around the round table

Birthday presents

1

2

3

Clocking off

12

9   3

6

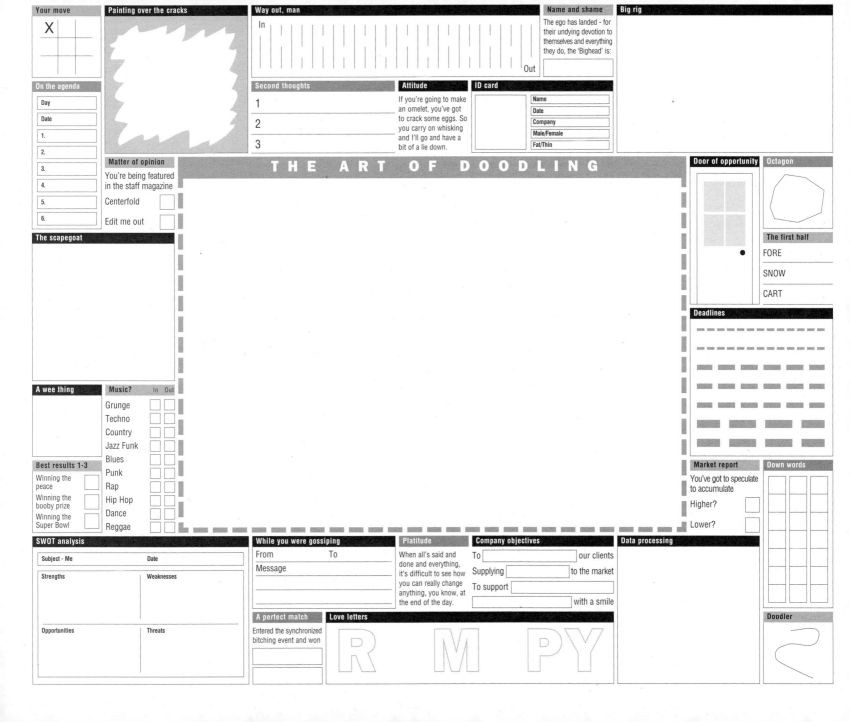

Your move

X

Painting over the cracks

Way out, man

In

Out

Name and shame

The ego has landed - for their undying devotion to themselves and everything they do, the 'Bighead' is:

Big rig

On the agenda

Day

Date

1.

2.

3.

4.

5.

6.

Second thoughts

1

2

3

Attitude

If you're going to make an omelet, you've got to crack some eggs. So you carry on whisking and I'll go and have a bit of a lie down.

ID card

| Name |
| Date |
| Company |
| Male/Female |
| Fat/Thin |

Matter of opinion

You're being featured in the staff magazine

Centerfold

Edit me out

THE ART OF DOODLING

Door of opportunity

Octagon

The first half

FORE

SNOW

CART

The scapegoat

Deadlines

A wee thing

Music?   In Out

Grunge

Techno

Country

Jazz Funk

Blues

Punk

Rap

Hip Hop

Dance

Reggae

Best results 1-3

Winning the peace

Winning the booby prize

Winning the Super Bowl

Market report

You've got to speculate to accumulate

Higher?

Lower?

Down words

SWOT analysis

Subject - Me	Date
Strengths	Weaknesses
Opportunities	Threats

While you were gossiping

From   To

Message

A perfect match

Entered the synchronized bitching event and won

Platitude

When all's said and done and everything, it's difficult to see how you can really change anything, you know, at the end of the day.

Company objectives

To _____ our clients

Supplying _____ to the market

To support _____

_____ with a smile

Data processing

Love letters

R M PY

Doodler

Moonlighting

Triangles

The domino effect

Reverse order 3-1

Losing the will to live

Losing your patience

Losing 50 bucks on the horses

Eureka

Robo husband patent

Title

Invented by

Working drawings

Signed

Mismatched

The extreme Republican and the extreme Democrat

Vice

She was finally done for third degree make-up, filing while under the influence of Cosmopolitan, and typing without due care and attention.

Carrot and stick

Re-branding

A BLANK CANVAS

Word association

Motivation

Criminal

Pineapple

Frenzy

Staff vote

A 3-hour daily limit on personal web surfing

You bet

No way

Today's big thing

After considering all the available options, it has been decided that the mammal of the day is:

A full and frank exchange of views - The phone call

Me | Other Person

Me | Other Person

Me | Other Person

Coffee Shops

1

2

3

Another re-organization

Window

Window

Door

Desk Chair Fold Up Bed Plant Me

Things shown half size

Advice

All you need to do in life is have a bit of talent, practice in the park for 16 hours a day, and over a period of years become a complete sporting icon. OK?

Twister

Media analysis

Possessions

Thriller

Rumours

Eagles Greatest

Led Zeppelin IV

The Bodyguard

The White Album

Come on Over

The Wall

Billy Joel Greatest

Back in Black

All the angles

Short straw

Flat broke

Key proposal

The implementation of a bad hair day

Lack of support

Total support

Pen-pushing

Start

Finish

Cause and effect

Blushing and concealing an embarrassed smile

Missing work and staying in bed all day

How many?

Ties

Badges

Pockets

Over the rainbow

Urgent status update

Name

Age | Hungry

Sex | Thirsty

Date | Desperate

Shapely shapes

Ridiculous names

1 _____
2 _____
3 _____

Small change

Favorite-comedic-moment screen grab

3 cities

_ _ _ _ _ _ _

_ _ _ _ _ _ _

_ _ _ _ _ _ _

The aerial view

Little jobs

Emptying the contents of your hole punch onto your desk and fashioning them into a geographical feature, before sneezing violently all over them.

Raw materials

Next week's forecast

Output

Mon Tues Wed Thurs Fri Sat Sun

New policies

Bringing your pet to work for a trial period

Agree ☐

Disagree ☐

Don't jump

RANDOM THOUGHTS

Appointments

It is with great pleasure that we announce that the position of the next office sneak goes to:

More accurate brand descriptions

The fruit pie that's actually full of fruit

The newspaper that has an element of news

The insurance policy with no get out clause

Pig or Duck

	P	D
Porker	☐	☐
Crispy	☐	☐
Mallard	☐	☐
Pot Bellied	☐	☐
Donald	☐	☐
Suckling	☐	☐
Greedy	☐	☐
Smelly	☐	☐
Look Out!	☐	☐
Peking	☐	☐

The low down

Italian?

Appetizer
_____

Main Course
_____

_____

Dessert

Colleagues in conflict

_____ V _____
_____ V _____
_____ V _____
_____ V _____

Time and motion

Trips to the bathroom ☐

Snacks gorged before lunch ☐

Breaks for long, lazy chats ☐

Window to the future

The big offensive idea

Whistle-blowing

Running an escort service in HR

Acceptable ☐

Not acceptable ☐

Dress code

Yesterday
_____

Today
_____

Tomorrow

It's a jungle out there

Dirty words

S X

Big jobs

What we need to do is get everybody to agree on everything, have enough food, never need to work, and still have change from 5 bucks.

Twins

Lively, interested, and willing to help if needed

After the tone - Your stalker

Message.................................
....
....
....

Little boxes

☐

☐

Airbrushed out

Junk mail

Any request that is looking for a volunteer

In tray

Out tray

You said that?

The Mall

Get ahead

Set an example to all by ordering a chair which is so adjustable in height that you can also undertake maintenance work on the light fittings.

Ten green bottles

A message from outer space

Remember to

_____

_____

_____

Singles dating search

Enter key elements that will assist your search

Results of search

Achievements

Mini victories won

Particularly funny jokes told

Emails sent before lunch

On the wagon

WHATEVER!

Lists of six

Things that aren't what they used to be

Irrelevant icon

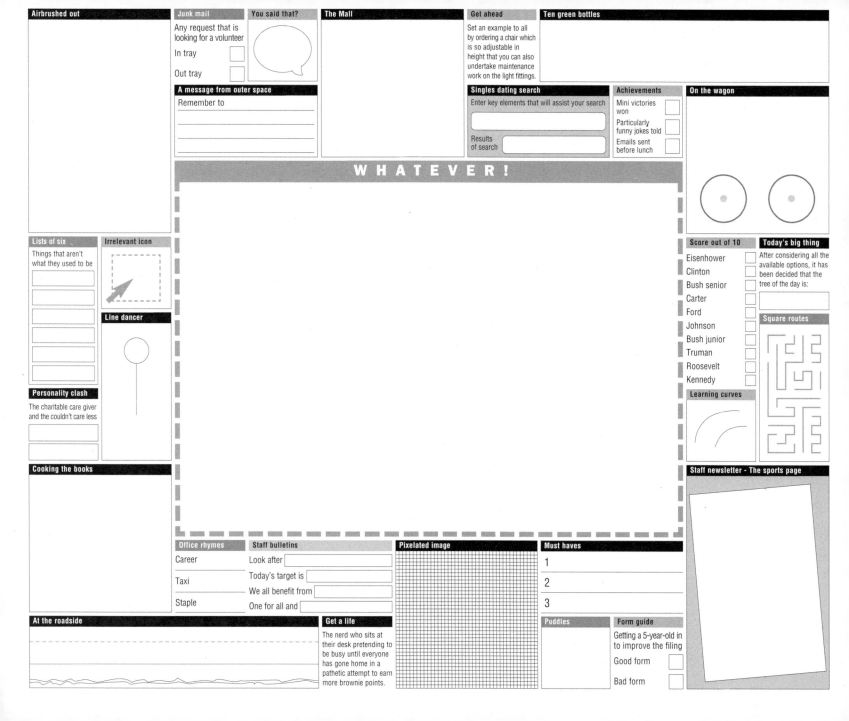

Line dancer

Personality clash

The charitable care giver and the couldn't care less

Cooking the books

At the roadside

Score out of 10

Eisenhower

Clinton

Bush senior

Carter

Ford

Johnson

Bush junior

Truman

Roosevelt

Kennedy

Learning curves

Today's big thing

After considering all the available options, it has been decided that the tree of the day is:

Square routes

Staff newsletter - The sports page

Office rhymes

Career

Taxi

Staple

Staff bulletins

Look after

Today's target is

We all benefit from

One for all and

Pixelated image

Must haves

1

2

3

Get a life

The nerd who sits at their desk pretending to be busy until everyone has gone home in a pathetic attempt to earn more brownie points.

Puddles

Form guide

Getting a 5-year-old in to improve the filing

Good form

Bad form

Life in a goldfish bowl

Professional opinion

Underworked, overpaid, and don't know they're born

Nasty, vicious, and worth having on your side

More interested in talking about it than doing it

Short shrift

Nice figures

695

Targets

Cars in the garage

Weeks off per year

Highest pinball score

Incident report

Name

Location

Who was there

What happened (in your own words)

Shape up

Corporate gift

To recognize your excellent contribution

Laptop

Lap Dancer

Eccentric plumbing

Golden hello

If you met your idol,

your opening words would be

GET THE DOODLE BUG

The big drop

Three witches

Two scribbles

Poison

Ivy

Dining

Yes, I think I'll have the pan-fried monkfish in a raspberry coulis with a terrine of fresh garden vegetables ... or maybe just a cheeseburger.

Whining

Well, I've had this pain in my lower back and now it's moved to the side, my head feels like it's about to explode, and, oh, my poor old feet.

Anxiety level

Been there?   Yes   No

Spain

Mexico

Canada

Italy

Ireland

Israel

China

Japan

Cuba

England

Post-It Note

Headquarters

The most pushy insurance salesman who ever sold you a policy

Hierarchy

The weekend

Ideal company for a weekend break

Patsy Cline

Kevin Kline

Together forever

Mr. and Mrs. Moaner from the pits of hell

Bed and breakfast

Dexterity test - Copying shapes

Bad hair

Endorsements

To promote the values of wildly irresponsible, manic, and antisocial behavior, let's hear it for:

Dream jobs

1

2

3

Geek chic

Baptism of fire

Today's big thing
After considering all the available options, it has been decided that the college of the day is:

Cartoon strip - The medical emergency

In the box

Your move
O

Expense claim - The hospitality evening
1.		$
2.		$
3.		$
4.		$
Total		$

Hardware
What we need is an alarm that gently wakes us with compliments and felicitations, then fills the bathtub and makes the breakfast.

Famous last words
1
2
3

Must do's
| Day |
| Date |
| 1. |
| 2. |
| 3. |
| 4. |
| 5. |
| 6. |

Octagon

Filing files

GIANT WHITE SPACE

Horoscope
Today, those close to you will find you:

very lively

in the bathroom

The second half
SPIN
LINE
SICK

Point of sale

Flower power

Preferences 1-10
Diner
Food Court
Cafe
Greasy Spoon
Coffee Shop
Fast-Food Outlet
Supper Club
Deli
Sandwich Shop
Restaurant

Tiny dress

Up words

Typing erors
The Employment Agency offered us the:

pick of the bunch

prick of the bunch

A fine record
Minutes from home to work
Drinks in a lunchtime
Weeks out sick

Deep throat

Ambitions beyond reason
Walking to
Living in
Making a
Pulling

Software
The installation of the 'Oh, I didn't see you there' program will inform you ten seconds before your boss looks over your shoulder.

While you were having a long lunch
From   To
Message

On the back of the party invitation

Doodler

Buzzwords
FP   HM

It'll never last
The fashion guru and the patently underdressed

Facial expressions - Excited

Tonight's pursuits

1

2

3

Bored meeting

Things were not quite as good as the shareholders hoped when the financial director shouted:

Abbrev.

SPA

BOB

MWA

PLV

Gazing out of the window

Seeing in the dark

Place names - The nearest place to hell on earth

The new recruit

We're getting a new guy to do our artwork

Mr. Dismal

Mr. Disney

Chain of command

Triangles

Twister

S

Good practice

To keep in with the girls, don't spend hours in front of the mirror, don't avoid any work in case you break a nail, and don't try to get all the male attention.

The numbers game

Wheels on your wagon

Calories in your lunch

Pens in your pocket

D R A W I N G   R O O M

Full page ad

Exploded view

A thermonuclear device

Checked   Signed

Four numbers

Like it?   Yes   No

Matthew

Andrew

Joseph

Michael

Ethan

Daniel

Joshua

Christopher

Anthony

Jacob

Bad practice

While in a drunken stupor on some foreign beach, send a cheerful and comprehensive postcard telling your colleagues what you think of them.

Opposites attract

The much bigger and the much smaller

Short head

Pen-pushing

Start

Finish

Qualifications

Essential if you want to get on with the CEO

Team Player

Poker Player

Low-loader

Mark up

One moment in time

Time	Date

Who's not in

Who's in blue

Who's eating

Seascape

How many?

Mirrors

Stars

Times

Putting it more bluntly

Advising staff of the importance of punctuality

Emphasizing the importance of efficiency

Question

Why is it that the day that starts with you forgetting the 16-digit door security code ends with the coffee machine emptying its contents into your lap?

Amazing space

Joyful texting

Captured on sitcom TV

Small fry

Excuses for sneaking out for an interview

1

2

3

Shapely shapes

Hiring and firing

The extrovert who insists 'I'm mad'

Hire

Fire

Caffeine count

Input

Mon Tues Wed Thurs Fri Sat Sun

Collateral damage

Road to nowhere

Today's big thing

After considering all the available options, it has been decided that the superhero of the day is:

Score out of 10

March

November

June

February

September

May

December

July

January

August

FREESTYLE DOODLING AREA

Descriptive descriptions

(n) A ball pen that has leaked in your pocket

(adj) Having to grab lunch between meetings

(v) Catching your sleeve on the door handle

Unreal reference

This confirms that

has performed

Signed

A very long way

Running order 1-3

Running it by the boss

Running out of good ideas

Running the country

Jousting jobs

V

V

V

V

Surfing the web

Word up

H E

The hard sell

Brainstorming

A competition to improve staff morale

Two thumbs up

Two fingers up

Attitude

Yesterday

Today

Tomorrow

Misshaped cookies

Boxed up

Break up voicemail

Message...................
....
....
....

Apples and oranges

The bright reddest and the pale yellowist

Answer

We're going to have to let you go because your personal skills do not meet our competency profile - and your name was drawn out of this box.

Things have gone a bit flat

Polished portal

Office gossip
If rumors are to be believed, the colleague who'd give you the best 'night out' would be:

Office sports

Slam dunk
in the basket

Important notices

Meeting
If anyone suggests a breakfast meeting come prepared with a pen, a laptop, some pancakes, maple syrup, a few eggs, and dressed in a robe.

Top three excuses
It fell over all on its own

I meant to save it, not send it

I don't do that sort of thing

Pole to pole

American Graffiti

Played It?
Yes No

Cribbage

Old Maid

Poker

Solitaire

Bridge

Uno

Blackjack

Spades

Rummy

Hearts

Learning curves

Girl talk

Market research
Quicker ways to leave the office

Fireman's Pole

Huge Slide

Useless notes about the shopping
Remember to

Calendar

THE BIG PICTURE

A squashy insect

Half woman

Lists of six
Things that feel rather pleasant to the touch

Made for each other
Marooned on a remote desert island together

Gap in the market

People to have an affair with
1
2
3

Caught in the act
Drunk in charge of your desk

Not guilty

Not coherent

Poop scoop

Spreadsheet

Error messages
Remove

Font clash

Wipe disk

Open up, then

Greeting
Usher potential new clients into a meeting room and treat them to a relaxing massage before giving them an offer they can't refuse.

Office rhymes
Mouse

Typo

Lamp

Over the hills and far away

The Big Apple

Shape up

Health and safety

To be used in the event of an emergency

Fire escape

Time travel

Assertiveness course

Name

Problem

Participant's need

Result

Order of merit 1-3

A day at the races

A day doing the decorating

A day being very sick

Job descriptions

Strutting about all day in a florescent vest

Lousing everything up and then moving on

Staring at a screen ignoring everything

Numbers racket

937

Short fuse

The back of a bus

Three dorks

The high life

Today's diary

8:26am - 9:13am

3:42pm - 3:54pm

9:15pm - 10:00pm

Worth doing

If you intend working late make sure everybody knows by setting up an encampment around your workstation and floodlighting the area.

Get out!

Director of short shrift and brief, unsympathetic treatment

MY SPACE

Unbelievable perk

A special slush fund of

$

has been set up for

The rat race

Not worth doing

Aiming for the highest standards of excellence, competence, or specialism in the belief that it will make you indispensable to the company.

Preferences 1-10

Citizen Kane

Singin' in the Rain

The Graduate

Gone with the Wind

On the Waterfront

Schindler's List

The Wizard of Oz

Casablanca

The Godfather

Lawrence of Arabia

Making your mark

Lean thinking

Today's big thing

After considering all the available options, it has been decided that the country of the day is:

Dexterity test - Joining numbers

1   26   5   96
6   73   8
48   3   87   4

High points

1

2

3

Lunch break

12
9   3
6

Outsourcing

Response time

If the finger of blame is pointed at you

Accept it

Point back

Bitter rivals

Citrus fruits that are particularly sharp

Seating plan

Your move

On the agenda

Day
Date
1.
2.
3.
4.
5.
6.

Through the fog

A very, very long way out

In _____

_____

_____

_____

Out _____

What else could you be doing?

1 _____

2 _____

3 _____

Attitude

You come here with your fancy, new fangled ideas, implying that we don't have the tools for the job. For the last time we don't need a photocopier.

Backstage pass

Name
Date
Gig
Visiting
Excited?   Yes   No

Name and shame

Known for going on and on and on and on and on and on and on and on and on and on and on:

Outdoor pursuits

Matter of opinion

Headquarters has been moved to Ireland

Bring it on ☐

I'm staying put ☐

THE ART OF DOODLING

Offshore deposits

A minuscule thing

Wet or dry   W   D

River ☐ ☐
Battery ☐ ☐
Drip ☐ ☐
Powder ☐ ☐
Monsoon ☐ ☐
Shave ☐ ☐
Atmosphere ☐ ☐
Desert ☐ ☐
Look ☐ ☐
Liquid ☐ ☐

Best results 1-3

Winning the voters confidence ☐

Winning a Tony Award ☐

Winning the space race ☐

Back door

Hexagon

The first half

WIND

FLAT

INTER

Line dancing

Market report

The most effective advertising slogan

Just do it ☐

Don't do it ☐

Down words

SWOT analysis

Subject - Last Week	Date
Strengths	Weaknesses
Opportunities	Threats

While you were looking out of the window

From _____   To _____

Message _____

_____

Platitude

If you'd left at 3, you could have got the 3:20 from Grand Central, changed after seventeen stations, and arrived precisely 7 minutes earlier.

Company objectives

To reap the rewards of _____

Becoming _____ within 5 years

We're here to _____

Your call is _____ to us

Time stamp

A perfect match

Joint winners of the complete jerk competition

Letter by letter

W K C R

Doodler

Silhouette

Triangles

Hopscotch

Reverse order 3-1
- Losing when you should have won
- Losing the plot completely
- Losing the argument

Eureka
New coffeemaker patent

Title

Invented by

Working drawings

Signed

Mismatched
The openly gay and the avowed heterosexual

Vice
Taking the headache tablet had prompted a pill popping, line snorting, illicit substance fest that put everybody in jail for six months.

Raising the alarm

Exit strategy

A BLANK CANVAS

Low cut

Cause and effect
Stomping around having a go at everyone

Drinking too much and smoking 40 a day

How many?
Briefs

Boxers

Bras

Mirage

Word association
- Centipede
- Brilliant
- Squelchy
- Rotund

Staff vote
Relaying personal phone calls over the speaker

You bet

No way

Today's big thing
After considering all the available options, it has been decided that the insect of the day is:

A full and frank exchange of views - The conference call

Me	Person 1
Me	Person 2
Person 3	Me
Person 1	Me
Person 2	Somebody else
Person 1	Me

Favorite people
1

2

3

Key proposal
Adding vodka to the water dispenser

Lack of support

Total support

Pen-pushing
Start

Finish

After the Feng Shui consultant
Door

Window

Bar Unit   Chair   Booze   Bin   Me

Things shown half size

Advice
You need to change your name to something Italian, check out a few color charts, and become one of the top fashion designers in the world. OK?

Twister

Organic growth

Possessions
- Trivial Pursuit
- Scrabble
- Chutes & ladders
- Pictionary
- Risk
- Go Fish
- Backgammon
- Scene It?
- Monopoly
- Twister

All the angles

Short tempered

Urgent status update

Name	
Age	Tired?
Sex	Emotional?
Date	Time to go home?

Shapely shapes	Nicknames	Smallpox	Real-life-disaster screen grab	3 things	Wonderwall	Little jobs

Shapely shapes

Nicknames

1

2

3

Smallpox

Real-life-disaster screen grab

3 things

_ _ _ _ _ _

_ _ _ _ _ _

_ _ _ _ _ _

Wonderwall

Little jobs

The very minor but critical re-organization of the desk which takes most of the morning but frees up space for an extra pile of unfinished stuff.

Bits and bytes

A weak end

Quality

Mon Tues Wed Thurs Fri Sat Sun

New policies

Holding a hoedown every Tuesday at 10

Agree

Disagree

The grapevine

RANDOM THOUGHTS

Appointments

It is with great pleasure that we announce that the position of the next office bore goes to:

More accurate brand descriptions

The breakfast cereal with plenty of added salt

The free gift that is of some practical use

The parcel service that delivers goods intact

Down or Out   D   O

Cast

Stay

Stairs

Wit

Pour

Work

Right

Smart

Load

Size

Falling down

Mexican night

Appetizer

Main Course

Dessert

Celebrity sparring

V

V

V

V

Time and motion

Visits to the doctor

Seconds to go

Trips to the bar

Window dressing

The big crazy idea

Whistle-blowing

Using a flamethrower to improve the décor

Acceptable

Not acceptable

Party plan

Dirty words

T   T

Big jobs

Our new work/life-balancing, personal, harmonizing, lifestyle-enhancing guru is here to ensure that we never feel stressed ever again, ever.

Spirit

Yesterday

Today

Tomorrow

Twins

Wasteful, difficult, and totally exasperating

After the tone - Ex boyfriend

Message..

....

....

....

....

Little boxes

Stairway to Heaven

Junk mail

The Management's idea of a staff day out

In tray

Out tray

The message you didn't get

Remember to

You don't say!

Macy's Parade

Get ahead

Clear your desk by throwing everything out of the window then offer to rent out space to those who have far too much on theirs.

Flat out

Research searching

Enter key elements that will assist your search

Results of search

Achievements

Bucks passed elsewhere

Fantastic deals closed

Flying pigs seen

Wheels in motion

WHATEVER!

Lists of six

Things that come back to haunt you

Rude icon

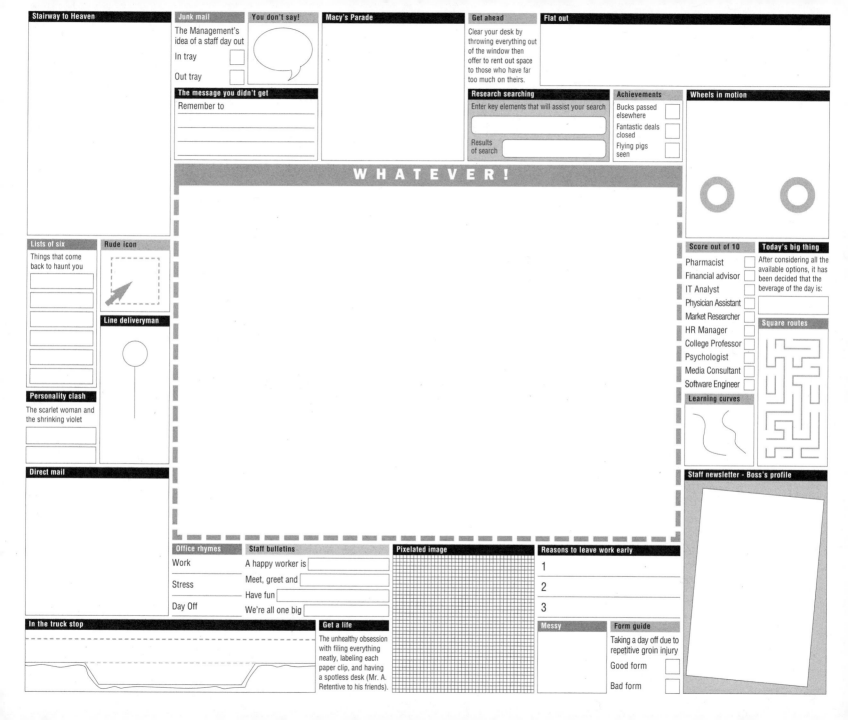

Line deliveryman

Personality clash

The scarlet woman and the shrinking violet

Direct mail

Score out of 10

Pharmacist

Financial advisor

IT Analyst

Physician Assistant

Market Researcher

HR Manager

College Professor

Psychologist

Media Consultant

Software Engineer

Learning curves

Today's big thing

After considering all the available options, it has been decided that the beverage of the day is:

Square routes

Staff newsletter - Boss's profile

Office rhymes

Work

Stress

Day Off

Staff bulletins

A happy worker is

Meet, greet and

Have fun

We're all one big

Pixelated image

Reasons to leave work early

1

2

3

In the truck stop

Get a life

The unhealthy obsession with filing everything neatly, labeling each paper clip, and having a spotless desk (Mr. A. Retentive to his friends).

Messy

Form guide

Taking a day off due to repetitive groin injury

Good form

Bad form

Bowl half empty or half full

Professional opinion
Not worth considering in any way, shape, or form

Everything you'd expect and more with bells on

Arrogant, self-opinionated, and with no purpose

Short position

Targets
Marshmallows in the mouth

Shots for 18 holes of golf

Masts on your boat

Figure it out
853

Disturbance report
Name

Location

Who was there

What happened (in your own words)

Shape up

Corporate gift
To keep you in your new position

Stock options

Stock car

Visualization exercise

GET THE DOODLE BUG

Fantasy partner
Until further notice this permit enables

to be seen with

Whining
Something needs to be done about our working environment: the floor's too flat, the corridor's full of air, the doors are blue, and the flowers smell.

Good or bad G B
Desirable

Unpleasant

Enjoyable

Arrogant

Beneficial

Naughty

Behavior

Vengeful

Expedient

Wicked

Post-It Note

Rage level

Drop zone

Three slobs

Two scribbles
Swing

Bridge

Dining
I think Catering should have been advised about the strong vegetarian element in the overseas delegation before suggesting a hog roast.

Headquarters
The kind of realtor who will happily sell you an igloo in Hawaii

---

A good set up

The weekend
An energy-sapping couple of days ahead

Paintballing

Paintstripping

Together forever
Mr. and Mrs. Devious from Deception City

Arms dealing

Dexterity test - Copying numbers
6 → 9 →

3 → 2 →

Face off
12

9   3

6

Endorsements
To promote the values of embarrassingly false interest in other people's lives, let's hear it for:

Unique selling points
1

2

3

Animal behavior

Awesome

Today's big thing

After considering all the available options, it has been decided that the ideology of the day is:

Cartoon strip - The Pickup

In the trash

Your move

O

Expense claim - The bonding course

1.	$
2.	$
3.	$
4.	$
Total	$

Hardware

All we need is a small handheld device that allows us to transform into a gas and then rematerialize in any chosen destination.

Honest brokers

1

2

3

Must do's

| Day |
| Date |
| 1. |
| 2. |
| 3. |
| 4. |
| 5. |
| 6. |

Hexagon

Closet love

GIANT WHITE SPACE

Horoscope

Don't take too much on today because:

you need a break

you're being fired

The second half

FOOD

BALL

NET

The tree of life

Research and development

Up words

Typing erors

Appointment made from a crackly dictation tape

An economist

A con artist

Preferences 1-10

Tom Hanks
Marlon Brando
Cary Grant
Robert DeNiro
Humphrey Bogart
Dustin Hoffman
James Stewart
Harrison Ford
Jack Nicholson
Henry Fonda

A tiny amount

A fine record

Hours for the marathon

Plastic cups thrown out

Important briefings ignored

Doodler

Touching base

Ambitions beyond reason

Entering

Winning the

Building a

Wasting some

Software

Click on the small, odd thing and at the gizmo-type prompt choose the Stuff option which enables you to do that clever thing with your screen.

While you were getting the coffees

From   To

Message

On the back of junk mail

Word processing

CH G A I

It'll never last

The celebrity couple whose faces turn your stomach

Facial expressions - Dead beat

Executive toys

1

2

3

Bored meeting

The meeting descended into complete and utter farce after the president had screamed out:

Jarring jargon

NOB

STG

CCX

PUA

A major incident

Night vision

Place names - The winner of most boring town award

The new recruit

Choice for the new boss of stock trading

Ms. Bull

Mr. Bear

Chain of command

Triangles

The numbers game

Letters in your name

The 1,000th digit of pi

Favorite odd number

Twister

Good practice

After a training course involving role play, continue in the most challenging role, that of the crazed, shrieking, and naked half man, half raccoon.

DRAWING ROOM

Exploded view

The Universe

Checked

Signed

In at the deep end

Four shapes

Like them? Yes No

Eggs

Chicken

Seafood

Peanuts

Pork

Blueberries

Tomatoes

Turkey

Apples

Rice

Short odds

Bad practice

Organize a pool for the number of weeks the boss will last following the discovery of some compromising photos, and ask him to join in.

Opposites attract

The really noisy and the very much more quiet

Electrical appliances

Pen-pushing

Start

Finish

Qualifications

Key skills necessary to fight for a job

Use a punch

Take a punch

Lowlife

One moment in time

Time		Date
Who's not up to it		
Who's whistling		
Who's farted		

The ocean wave

How many?

Hats

Flags

Scarves

Putting it more bluntly

Outlining the new management structure

Suggesting an important company-away day

Question

Why is it that a character-building learning experience inevitably leads to impossible targets, mind-boggling pressure, and complete burn out?

The right path

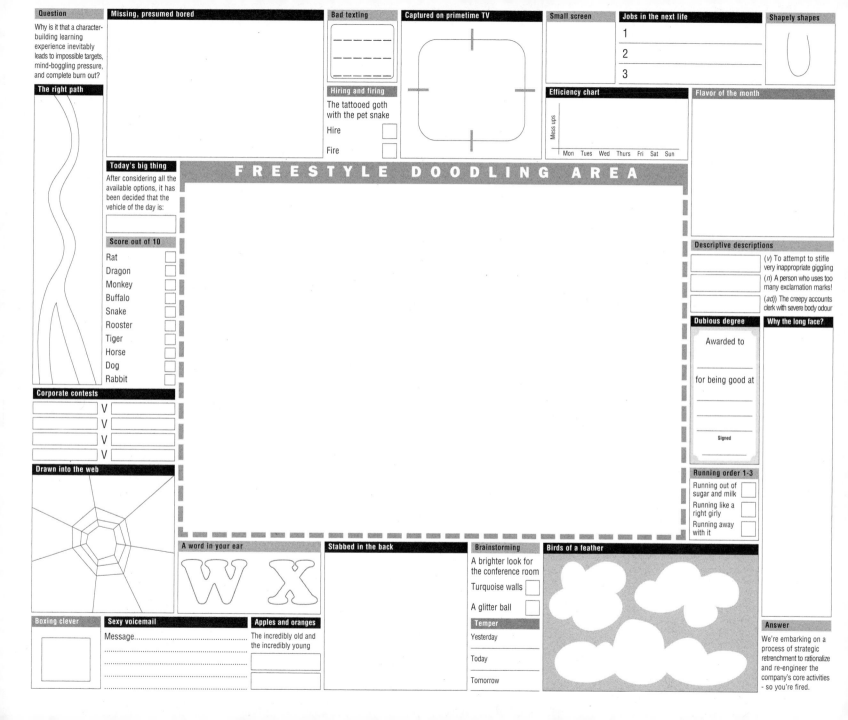

Today's big thing

After considering all the available options, it has been decided that the vehicle of the day is:

Score out of 10

Rat
Dragon
Monkey
Buffalo
Snake
Rooster
Tiger
Horse
Dog
Rabbit

Corporate contests

V
V
V
V

Drawn into the web

Boxing clever

Missing, presumed bored

Bad texting

Captured on primetime TV

Small screen

Jobs in the next life

1
2
3

Shapely shapes

Hiring and firing

The tattooed goth with the pet snake

Hire

Fire

Efficiency chart

Mess ups

Mon Tues Wed Thurs Fri Sat Sun

Flavor of the month

FREESTYLE DOODLING AREA

Descriptive descriptions

(v) To attempt to stifle very inappropriate giggling

(n) A person who uses too many exclamation marks!

(adj) The creepy accounts clerk with severe body odour

Dubious degree

Awarded to

for being good at

Signed

Why the long face?

Running order 1-3

Running out of sugar and milk

Running like a right girly

Running away with it

A word in your ear

W X

Sexy voicemail

Message..
....
....
....

Apples and oranges

The incredibly old and the incredibly young

Stabbed in the back

Brainstorming

A brighter look for the conference room

Turquoise walls

A glitter ball

Temper

Yesterday

Today

Tomorrow

Birds of a feather

Answer

We're embarking on a process of strategic retrenchment to rationalize and re-engineer the company's core activities - so you're fired.

Lying low

Meeting
To ensure that the vital emergency sales meeting finishes in time for the usual trip to the bar, provide a ten minute warning by bullhorn.

Natural wastage

Baby talk

Market research
Most embarrassing time at the top
Bush Jnr.
Clinton

Think of your secretary

Red carpet treatment

Top three excuses
I was still in bed at the time
I thought he'd like it
I didn't realize it was still plugged in

Bridging the gap

Useless notes about the house
Remember to

THE BIG PICTURE

Office gossip
Apparently, the person everybody says is most likely to do anything for a few cents is:

Like/Dislike   L   D
Fast food
Live shows
Spikey hair
Italy
Skateboards
Large hats
Warm beer
Dogs
Thursdays
Slippers

Office sports

Get the thing in the circle

Learning curves

Theatre bulletin board

A scary insect

Lists of six
Places to keep the important little things

Hand signal

Made for each other
Would look good in each other's clothes

Money laundering

Earning money on the side
1
2
3

Set squares

Error messages
Corrupted
Re-insert lead
Overload in
For no reason

Office rhymes
Staff

Resign

Perk

Caught in the act
A quick grope behind the filing cabinet
A real handful
Missed again

Amoeba

Greeting
On a normal Monday morning, greet everybody as though they were long lost relatives. Leave work by 9:30am if the emotion overcomes you.

Rough ground

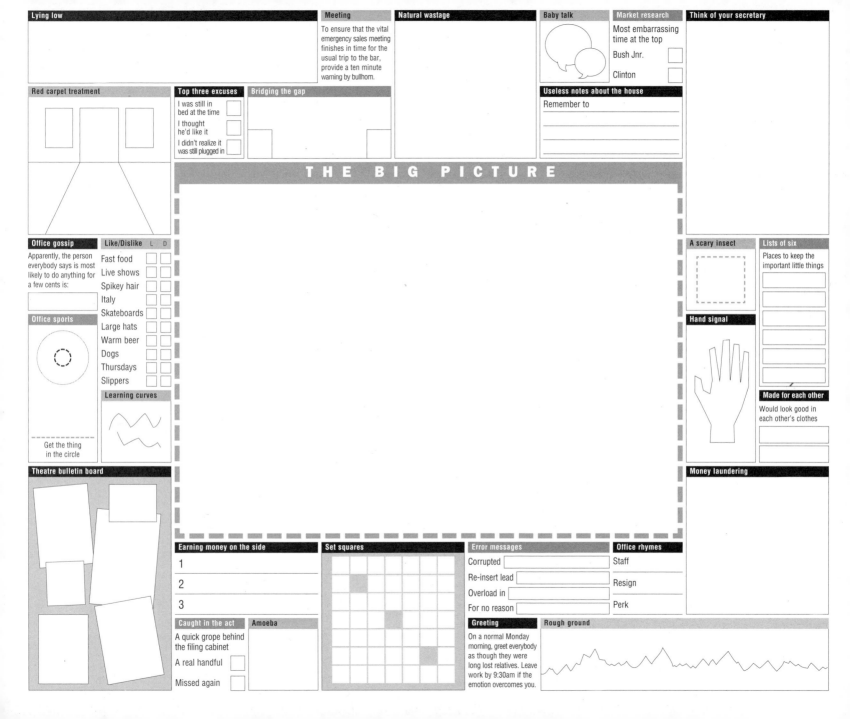

The big banana

Shape up

Harassment course

Name

Problem

How it will help

Result

Health and safety

Suitable gear for your next review

All suited up

Body armor

Order of merit 1-3

An evening in front of the TV

An evening on the town

An evening on Platform 7

Job descriptions

Walking around with three bits of paper

Criticizing everything that moves (or doesn't)

Having a very large piece of cake and eating it

Prime numbers

3 29

Shorthand

Park bench

MY SPACE

Three bitches

Download

Today's diary

4:12pm - 5:43pm

7:53pm - 10:34pm

Midnight - 5:15am

Worth doing

On a hot day, lay a large cooling fan down in a strategically selected place and try to recreate the Marilyn Monroe effect on your colleagues.

Out to lunch

Director of extreme cowardice and the inability to communicate

Fantasy air ticket

This ticket enables

to fly out, with a few pals, to

The space race

Not worth doing

Writing to a high ranking official in any large organization about a problem and awaiting a sensible reply that actually addresses the issue.

Preferences 1-10

☐ Rothko
☐ Monet
☐ Pollack
☐ Van Gogh
☐ Warhol
☐ Matisse
☐ Botticelli
☐ Dali
☐ Raphael
☐ Hirst

Favorite keys

Call Center

Today's big thing

After considering all the available options, it has been decided that the town of the day is:

Dexterity test - Grouping small blobs

Downsizing

Response time

If a very old, ignored memo is found

Blame the mail

Shred it

The exam room

Favorite movies

1

2

3

Coffee break

12
9   3
6

Bitter rivals

People with astonishing vested interests

Your move

X

On the agenda

| Day |
| Date |
| 1. |
| 2. |
| 3. |
| 4. |
| 5. |
| 6. |

Through the dirty window

One way or another

In

Out

Low points

1

2

3

Attitude

I know I only gave you half an hour to prepare the summary of the report I've been writing for months, but tell me why it isn't ready yet!

Exclusive viewing

| Name |
| Date |
| Film |
| Dress |
| Time |

Name and shame

Most likely to emerge from the bathroom with his zipper undone or her skirt tucked into her panties:

Flea market

Matter of opinion

A little light listening to brighten up the day

Military band

Heavy metal

One vision

A minute thing

Played it?

Yes   No

Pinball
Frisbee
Blackjack
Paintball
Craps
Charades
Poker Dice
Handball
Tic-tac-toe
Chess

Best results 1-3

Winning on the slot machines

Winning the next contract

Winning away on the weekend

THE ART OF DOODLING

Bathroom door

Polygon

The first half

BOOK

HAND

MULTI

Line management

Market report

The signal to urgently sell, sell, sell

Frantic arm waving

A shrill scream

Down words

SWOT analysis

Subject - The Refrigerator	Date
Strengths	Weaknesses
Opportunities	Threats

While you were filing your nails

From   To

Message

A perfect match

Competing for the title of Most Arrogant Dork

Red letter day

SKMWEI

Platitude

Well, I did say that you shouldn't have tried repairing it yourself, now the warranty's invalid and the whole lot is just a pile of smouldering rubble.

Company objectives

To _____ graduates

Creating _____ for the community

Having fun whilst _____

To value _____ extremely highly

Miniature golf

Doodler

Dancing in the dark

Triangles

Round things

Reverse order 3-1
Losing all sense of control
Losing the shirt off your back
Losing your direction

Eureka
New game patent
Title
Invented by
Working drawings
Signed

Mismatched
The incredibly tall and the unusually short

Vice
Apparently, he'd been found at midnight by a security guard hopping around in a pink latex rabbit suit nibbling at his leather desk diary.

Space travel

The sharp end

A BLANK CANVAS

Low fat

Cause and effect
Dumbstruck, bulging eyes, and rigidly still

Punching the air and performing cartwheels

How many?
Pets

Chins

Burgers

Word association
Boredom
Gerbil
Performance
Poke

Staff vote
A ban on discussing last night's TV

You bet

No way

Today's big thing
After considering all the available options, it has been decided that the fish of the day is:

A full and frank exchange of views - The heated conversation
Guy at the Bar   Me
Someone else   Me

Another person (not really involved)   Me

Drop dead gorgeous
1
2
3

Landscape

Key proposal
The introduction of a Very Loud Day

Lack of support

Total support

Pen-pushing
Start

Finish

Design for life
Door

Window

Water Bed   Chair   Wardrobe   Statue   Me
Things shown half size

Advice
You need to invent something, get your face plastered all over the media, and become an authority on being an entrepreneur. OK?

Twister

The life/work balance

Possessions
Robert Ludlum
Stephen King
Dan Brown
Michael Moore
Graham Greene
Roald Dahl
J. K. Rowling
Jackie Collins
Tom Clancy
D. H. Lawrence

All the angles

Short pants

Urgent status update
Name
Age   Height
Sex   Weight
Date   Shoe size

Shapely shapes

Big brands

1 _____

2 _____

3 _____

Small minded

Movie-romance screen grab

3 names

_ _ _ _ _ _

_ _ _ _ _ _

_ _ _ _ _ _

Out of bounds

Little jobs

Once you have dealt with the ass who put it there, embellish the coffee stain on the cover of your report into a clever, artistic feature.

Badge of honor

Current projection

Stuff

Mon Tues Wed Thurs Fri Sat Sun

New policies

A naughty corner for office bullies

Agree ☐

Disagree ☐

Career ladder

RANDOM THOUGHTS

Appointments

It is with great pleasure that we announce that the position of the next office weirdo goes to:

High or Low   H   L

	H	L
Bridge	☐	☐
Stakes	☐	☐
Life	☐	☐
Brow	☐	☐
Flier	☐	☐
Specification	☐	☐
Voice	☐	☐
Diver	☐	☐
Jinks	☐	☐
Cloud	☐	☐

More accurate brand descriptions

It keeps working until you get it home

It comes in kit form with one piece missing

It doesn't do exactly what it says on the tin

Don't look down

Favorites menu

Appetizer

Main Course

Dessert

Family fights

	V	
	V	
	V	
	V	

Through the smashed window

Time and motion

Mistakes before lunch ☐

Weekends worked this year ☐

Arguments during the day ☐

The big money-making idea

Whistle-blowing

Giving nicknames to senior management

Acceptable ☐

Not acceptable ☐

Demeanor

Yesterday

Today

Tomorrow

Doggie bag

Dirty words

N B

Big jobs

Of course, what we do is mirror life and provide a window on the world through which everyone can see themselves as they really are, do you see?

Twins

Totally dedicated to their respective causes

After the tone - Your boss

Message................................

....

....

....

Little boxes

☐   ☐

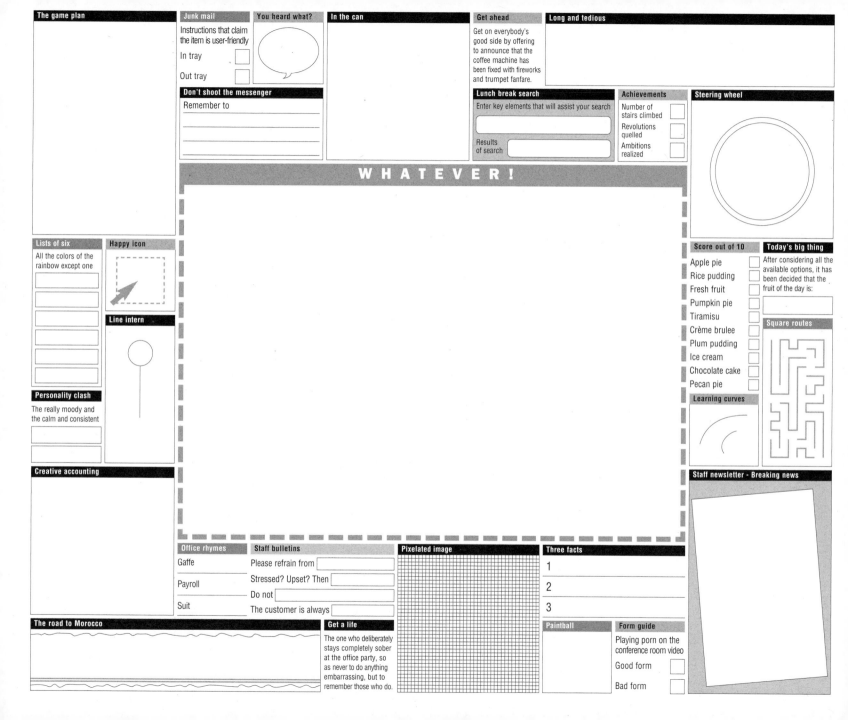

The game plan

Junk mail
Instructions that claim the item is user-friendly
In tray ☐
Out tray ☐

You heard what?

In the can

Get ahead
Get on everybody's good side by offering to announce that the coffee machine has been fixed with fireworks and trumpet fanfare.

Long and tedious

Don't shoot the messenger
Remember to

Lunch break search
Enter key elements that will assist your search

Results of search

Achievements
Number of stairs climbed ☐
Revolutions quelled ☐
Ambitions realized ☐

Steering wheel

WHATEVER!

Lists of six
All the colors of the rainbow except one

Happy icon

Line intern

Personality clash
The really moody and the calm and consistent

Creative accounting

Score out of 10
Apple pie ☐
Rice pudding ☐
Fresh fruit ☐
Pumpkin pie ☐
Tiramisu ☐
Crème brulee ☐
Plum pudding ☐
Ice cream ☐
Chocolate cake ☐
Pecan pie ☐

Learning curves

Today's big thing
After considering all the available options, it has been decided that the fruit of the day is:

Square routes

Staff newsletter - Breaking news

Office rhymes
Gaffe

Payroll

Suit

Staff bulletins
Please refrain from
Stressed? Upset? Then
Do not
The customer is always

Pixelated image

Three facts
1
2
3

The road to Morocco

Get a life
The one who deliberately stays completely sober at the office party, so as never to do anything embarrassing, but to remember those who do.

Paintball

Form guide
Playing porn on the conference room video
Good form ☐
Bad form ☐

Bonsai tree

Professional opinion
Worth every cent of their massive bonus

Sycophantic, groveling, and totally unnecessary

Lean, mean, and squeaky clean

Short circuit

Targets
Consecutive pots in pool

Homes in the country

Profiteroles for dessert

Figuratively speaking
1 1 4

Situation report
Name

Location

Who was there

What happened (in your own words)

Shape up

Corporate gift
In appreciation of your long and loyal service

Engraved pen

Engraved headstone

The airport

Fantasy house swap
Until further notice this permit enables

to turn up and live in

Whining
I'm much better than they say I am, I'm only late a few times a week, I get some things done eventually, and who needs a computer anyway?

Like them? Yes No
Germans

Russians

Italians

Mexicans

British

Canadians

French

Australians

Irish

Japanese

Post-It Note

Stress level

GET THE DOODLE BUG

Dropout

Three good guys

Two scribbles
Meter

Maid

Dining
So it's jambalaya, crawfish pie, and fillet gumbo, and we're going to have big fun on the bayou ... can't I stay home with a pizza?

Headquarters
The most crooked law practice that ever perverted the course of justice

Restructuring

The weekend
Celebrating the end of the week:

with the relatives

...not!

Together forever
Mr. and Mrs. Complete Idiot from How Thick Can You Get

Consultancy

Dexterity test - Copying patterns

Endorsements
To promote the values of profiteering at just about everybody else's expense, let's hear it for:

Cap in hand

Head up

The 'A' team
1

2

3

Arms dealing

Today's big thing

After considering all the available options, it has been decided that the profession of the day is:

Cartoon strip - Leading up to the fight

It's in the bag

Your move

O

Expense claim - Entertaining

1.	$
2.	$
3.	$
4.	$
Total	$

Hardware

All we need is a robot that does all the cleaning, washes and irons our clothes, then sorts out our social engagements without getting involved.

Catastrophic campaigns

1

2

3

Must do's

| Day |
| Date |
| 1. |
| 2. |
| 3. |
| 4. |
| 5. |
| 6. |

Polygon

Neatly filed

The second half

MARK

BOARD

EASY

Horoscope

You'll be the center of attention today because:

you're a Virgo

your hair sucks

Virtual organization

Flower of Scotland

GIANT WHITE SPACE

Up words

Typing erors

Sexual harassment has reduced since he left

Previous doorman

Pervious doorman

Preferences 1-10

Hannah
Abigail
Olivia
Isabella
Ava
Madison
Emily
Ashley
Samantha
Emma

Tiny pieces

A fine record

Years waiting for the perfect partner

Lengths done at the pool

Months without a driving conviction

System dump

Ambitions beyond reason

Flying a

Pushing over

Do better than

Perform

Software

If you were to reinstall the software, reboot, and then try the same procedure again, it's more than likely that the problem will still be there.

While you were stuck in the elevator

From   To

Message

On the back of a bill envelope

Doodler

Wordsmith

OTR NG

It'll never last

The most obviously talented and talentless

Facial expressions - Delirious

Fast cars

1

2

3

Bored meeting

It became apparent that the targets had to be the subject of further discussion when the sales director shouted:

Jargonese

NON

DDD

ZOM

BUB

Safe

Is that legal?

Place names - The state with the most incompetent governor

The new recruit

Say 'Hi' to our new bartender

Jack Daniels

Shirley Temple

Chain of command

Triangles

The numbers game

Useless things on your desk

Windows in the room

Sheets in the copier tray

Twister

Good practice

Every morning bring in a bunch of flowers and spread some love, peace, and understanding to all mankind, at least those in the immediate vicinity.

DRAWING ROOM

Photographic evidence

Exploded view

Warp speed

Checked   Signed

Four squiggles

Green/Yellow   G   Y

Field

Ribbon

Mile

Peril

Tree

Custard

Slime

Fever

Back

Berets

Short staffed

One moment in time

Time   Date

What's out the window

Who's wearing a hat

Who's not interested

Pen-pushing

Start

Finish

Qualifications

Basic requirements for the traveling salesman

Own car

Own teeth

Very low tide

Liquid assets

How many?

Pictures

Fans

Keys

Bad practice

Deciding to cancel 'dress down Wednesday' because of an extremely important visit by an overseas delegation and forgetting to tell everyone.

Opposites attract

The deepest and the terribly shallow

Cutting-edge knowledge

Putting it more bluntly

Asking for volunteers to collect for charity

Requesting offers for a little extra overtime

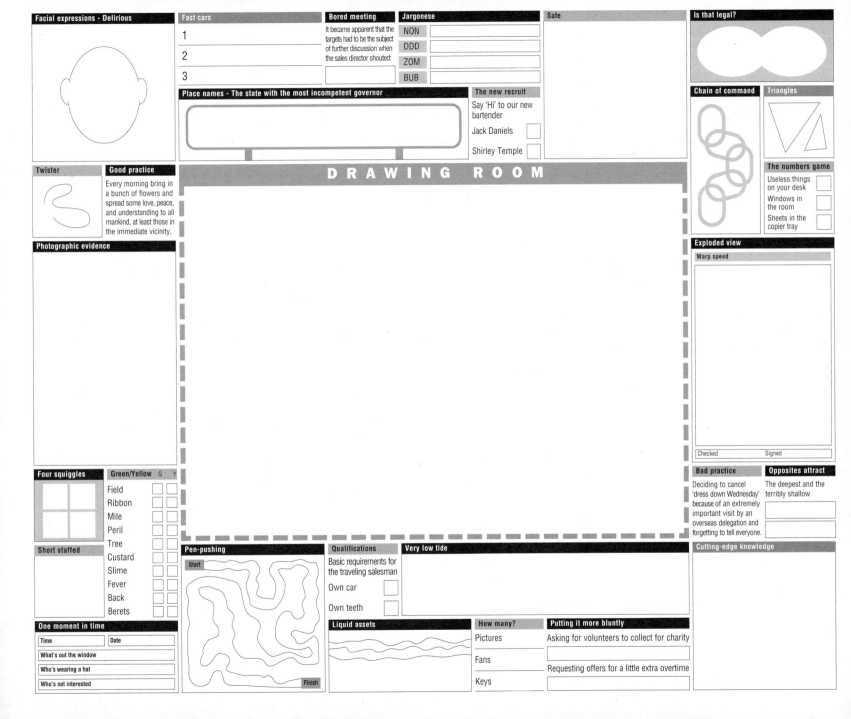

Question

What the hell is the difference between an aim and an objective, and where does a goal fit in, and don't get me started on missions and visions!

Picture this

Happy texting

Captured on drama TV

Small minded

Marvelous ideas

1
2
3

Shapely shapes

Road to ruin

Hiring and firing

The consultant known as 'The Grim Reaper'

Hire

Fire

Enthusiasm levels

Activity

Mon   Tues   Wed   Thurs   Fri   Sat   Sun

Raising the barrier

Today's big thing

After considering all the available options, it has been decided that the outlaw of the day is:

FREESTYLE DOODLING AREA

Score out of 10

Engineers
Architects
Doctors
Bankers
Hookers
Teachers
Lawyers
Financiers
Builders
Accountants

Descriptive descriptions

(v) Talking in fluent jargonese to sound clever

(adj) Feeling after a career-limiting experience

(n) Anyone who uses the term perceptual mapping

Tacky testimonial

Awarded to

for doing reasonably well at

Signed

A very long thing

Departmental competitions

V
V
V
V

Website

Running order 1-3

Running into a brick wall

Running with a large, heavy object

Running down the government

Words worth

V   T

Bulls and bears

Brainstorming

Making better use of the meeting room

Free massage

Latin bar

Misshaped monsters

All wrapped up

IRS voicemail

Message..
....
....
....

Apples and oranges

The very, very highest and the lowest of the low

Prospects

Yesterday

Today

Tomorrow

Answer

I'm sorry I'm unable to come to the phone as I'm bawling out some very junior member of staff, but please leave your message after the tone.

Slithering along

Posh porch

Office gossip

Despite no evidence to back this up, the person with the most 'interesting' private wardrobe is:

Office sports

Try and boot it through the posts

Fridge magnets

Meeting

To make the evening cooking roster more interesting, provide a white board interactive presentation on how to achieve total efficiency.

Top three excuses

I thought that it would rub off

It's never done that before

I thought it was Wednesday

Over the fence

Tried It?

	Yes	No
Kumquat		
Blueberry		
Papaya		
Avocado		
Huckleberry		
Pawpaw		
Crowberry		
Lychee		
Guava		
Pomegranate		

Learning curves

Covered wagon

THE BIG PICTURE

Moaners

1

2

3

Caught in the act

Going on holiday during a crisis

I'll cancel then

Who cares

Splat!

Squared up

Talk talk

Market research

Most relaxing background music

Panpipes

Bagpipes

Useless notes about tonight

Remember to

Error messages

Not enough

Select option

Error code

Please delete

Greeting

Next time you visit a customer with a highly polished wood floor in reception, take a good, long run up and come sliding in on your knees.

Multimedia

An itchy insect

Half and half

Lists of six

Things that go all moldy very quickly

Made for each other

Tied up together in a sack and put in the river

Focus group

Office rhymes

Clock

Phone

Sickie

Difficult terrain

The big one

Shape up

Health and safety
Measures to cut down on accidents

More vigilance

Inflatable floor

Advanced gibberish course
Name

Problem

Aim for participant

_____
_____
_____
_____
_____

Result

Order of merit 1-3
A box full of tissues

A box full of chocolates

A box full of badgers

Figures of fun
639

Job descriptions
Picking something up here and putting it over there

Making a very nice silk purse out of a pig's ear

Providing pathetic excuses for terrible services

Shortfall

On the throne

Three scumbags

Droppings

Today's diary
7:30am - 8:15am

2:47pm - 2:48pm

8:15pm - 9:00pm

Worth doing
If your building is a bit like a rabbit warren, or even if it isn't, lay down a salt trail every time you move from one department to another.

Do be coming inward
Director of over elaborate and dressed up language for no particular reason

MY SPACE

Fantasy lottery win
A special cash prize win of

$

has been won by

A rise to the top

Not worth doing
When a particularly popular colleague leaves, deciding to collect for a nice leaving present and expecting everybody to give you their contribution.

Preferences 1-10
- Monterey Jack
- Swiss
- Bergere Bleue
- Idaho Goatster
- Tillamook Cheddar
- Cougar Gold
- Peekskill Pyramid
- Brick
- Texas Goat
- Maytag Blue

Hallmark

Mergers and acquisitions

Today's big thing
After considering all the available options, it has been decided that the color of the day is:

Dexterity test - Joining letters
H M R O
W X Q
V P E Y

Big mistakes
1

2

3

Clocked
12
9   3
6

Blowing the bonus

Response time
If phoned at home when on a sickie

Pretend to be ill

Pretend to be out

Bitter rivals
Two people who really don't like each other

Table manners

Your move

X

On the agenda

| Day |
| Date |
| 1. |
| 2. |
| 3. |
| 4. |
| 5. |
| 6. |

Blot on the landscape

The long way out (or maybe the short way in)

In

Out

Name and shame

Loves the sound of their own voice but produces more hot air than the Montgolfier brothers:

Advertising billboard

Heavy hitters

1

2

3

Attitude

OK, I know we were the most expensive quote with the most persuasive and obnoxious sales team, but do you want us to do the job or not?

Hospital pass

| Name |
| Date |
| Condition |
| Symptoms |
| Color |

Matter of opinion

Becoming over friendly with a colleague

Depends

Too dangerous

THE ART OF DOODLING

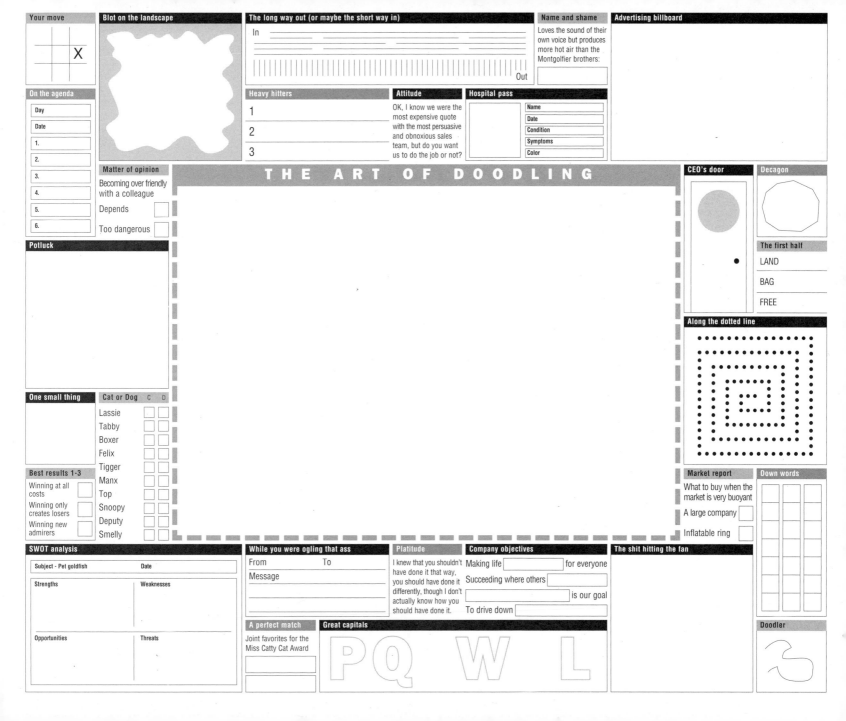

CEO's door

Decagon

The first half

LAND

BAG

FREE

Along the dotted line

Potluck

One small thing

Cat or Dog C D

Lassie
Tabby
Boxer
Felix
Tigger
Manx
Top
Snoopy
Deputy
Smelly

Best results 1-3

Winning at all costs

Winning only creates losers

Winning new admirers

Market report

What to buy when the market is very buoyant

A large company

Inflatable ring

Down words

SWOT analysis

Subject - Pet goldfish		Date	
Strengths		Weaknesses	
Opportunities		Threats	

While you were ogling that ass

From   To

Message

Platitude

I knew that you shouldn't have done it that way, you should have done it differently, though I don't actually know how you should have done it.

Company objectives

Making life ___ for everyone

Succeeding where others ___

___ is our goal

To drive down ___

The shit hitting the fan

A perfect match

Joint favorites for the Miss Catty Cat Award

Great capitals

P Q W L

Doodler

3

The dark side

Triangles

Juggling balls

Reverse order 3-1
Losing that nasty rash
Losing 5 bucks but finding 10
Losing a good night's sleep

Eureka
Robot boss patent
Title
Invented by
Working drawings

Signed

Mismatched
The all-action tough guy and the inactive wimp

Vice
Offering to take a client to the ball game then ending up in rehab with no recollection of where you went, having blown the entertainment budget.

The paper cut

Panic attack

Word association
Beetroot
Irritating
Wisdom
Exhilarating

Staff vote
Presenting a 'Last to arrive' award
You bet
No way

Today's big thing
After considering all the available options, it has been decided that the smell of the day is:

Far away destinations
1
2
3

A full and frank exchange of views - The appraisal
The Boss — Me
The Boss — Me
The Secretary — Me

A B L A N K C A N V A S

The beach hut layout
Window   Door

Deckchair   Ball   Bookshelf   Bucket   Me
Things shown half size

Advice
You need to start off as a political subversive, have a relatively minor brush with the law, stand for election, and become a people's champion. OK?

Twister

Boiler room

Possessions
Backstreet Boys
Foo Fighters
Moby
U2
Outkast
The Beach Boys
Aerosmith
The Corrs
Run DMC
The Strokes

All the angles

Shortwave

Low alcohol

Key proposal
Christmas decorations all year round
Lack of support
Total support

Pen-pushing
Start
Finish

Cause and effect
Collapsing on to the floor as a gibbering wreck
Waiting for the right opportunity for revenge

How many?
Lipsticks
Bags
Tweezers

Sunrise

Urgent status update
Name
Age — Need a break?
Sex — Need a haircut?
Date — Need a pee?

Shapely shapes

Favorite things
1
2
3

Small print

Incredible-sporting-moment screen grab

3 movies
_ _ _ _ _ _
_ _ _ _ _ _
_ _ _ _ _ _

On the big screen

Little jobs
During lunch, unpeel your orange so that the skin is in one piece, rework it into it's original shape, and leave it on top of your computer printer.

Inventory

Plotting the downfall
Targets
Mon Tues Wed Thurs Fri Sat Sun

New policies
Hold a weekly 'Vote off a colleague' show

Agree

Disagree

An outside elevator

R A N D O M   T H O U G H T S

Appointments
It is with great pleasure that we announce that the position of the next office geek goes to:

More accurate brand descriptions

It's likely to cause far more trouble than it's worth

You've got to have it even though there's no need for it

Working to keep everyone up to their neck in debt

Deeper and down

Haute cuisine
Appetizer

Main Course

Dessert

Like It?   Yes   No
Fire-Eater
Illusionist
Acrobat
Pole dancer
Unicyclist
Drag Artist
Ventriloquist
Clown
Escapologist
Mime Artist

Punchy politicians
V
V
V
V

Time and motion
Good ideas turned down

Miles from home

Doors closed in your face

Window on the world

The big impossible idea

Whistle-blowing
Taking bets on how long the new CEO will last

Acceptable

Not acceptable

The kindergarten

Dirty words
C   K

Big jobs
Why don't we create a huge conglomerate which offers everything to everybody - and then actually provide a good service as well?

Humor
Yesterday

Today

Tomorrow

Twins
Engaging, witty, and really good company

After the tone - Your hot date
Message.....................................
....
....
....

Little boxes

Economies of scale

Junk mail
An incentive scheme with no real incentive

In tray ☐

Out tray ☐

You said what?!

Fair competition

Get ahead
Getting noticed by senior management can happen in various ways, but perhaps turning up to work totally naked is taking things too far.

Danger - Low bridge

Message in a bottle
Remember to

Ideal partner search
Enter key elements that will assist your search

Results of search

Achievements
Obstacles overcome ☐

Weight gained in a week ☐

Minor sporting trophies won ☐

It's like riding a bike

WHATEVER!

Lists of six
Things not to touch without rubber gloves

Mad icon

Line convict

Personality clash
The extreme control freak and the subordinate

Coupling

The truck lane

Score out of 10
Sweet & Sour ☐
Pesto ☐
Chilli Sauce ☐
Bolognese ☐
Chasseur ☐
Pepper Sauce ☐
Tzatziki ☐
Hollandaise ☐
Barbeque Sauce ☐
Ragu ☐

Today's big thing
After considering all the available options, it has been decided that the building of the day is:

Square routes

Learning curves

Staff newsletter - Absolute scandal

Office rhymes
Text

Desk

Bus

Staff bulletins
We are the

Making the day

Doing this for

The company is

Pixelated image

Nights out
1

2

3

Get a life
Everyone deserves a vacation but preparing next year's expedition on the first day back after two weeks in Florida is asking for trouble.

Spilt milk

Form guide
Making a photocopy of your butt

Good form ☐

Bad form ☐

Rose Bowl

Professional opinion
Opportunists looking for someone's mess to clear up

Totally genuine and the very salt of the earth

Prepared to talk absolute rubbish in public

Shortage

Figure hugging
602

Targets
Guests at your party

Notches on the bedpost

Seconds for the 100 metres

Status report
Name

Location

Who was there

What happened (in your own words)

Shape up

Corporate gift
For your valued service to the company

Watch and chain

Ball and chain

Cartoon

Perverted behavior permit
Until further notice this permit allows

to be as perverted as they like and

Whining
If you're busy, she always thinks she's busier, if you're stressed, she's always even more stressed, and if you're sick, she's always at death's door.

Been there? Yes No
The Big Easy

Fog City

Philly

Beer City

Motor City

Mile-High City

Windy City

Beantown

The Big D

Emerald City

Post-It Note

Angst level

GET THE DOODLE BUG

Waterfall

Three bad guys

Two scribbles
Cottage

Cheese

Dining
Even after the six-course banquet given by headquarters to celebrate last year's figures, it's a must to grab a burger and fries on the way home.

Headquarters
The most infested of loan sharks who ever promised you the world

Networking

The weekend
To avoid a weekend of Do It Yourself

Pull a muscle

Pull a partner

Together forever
Mr. and Mrs. Sunshine from Somewhere over the Rainbow

Express mail

Dexterity test - Even by odd
7 → 3 →
1 → 9 →

Nice hat

Endorsements
To promote the benefits of a well-balanced, addiction- and excess-free lifestyle, let's hear it for:

Your State Governor

Great quarterbacks
1
2
3

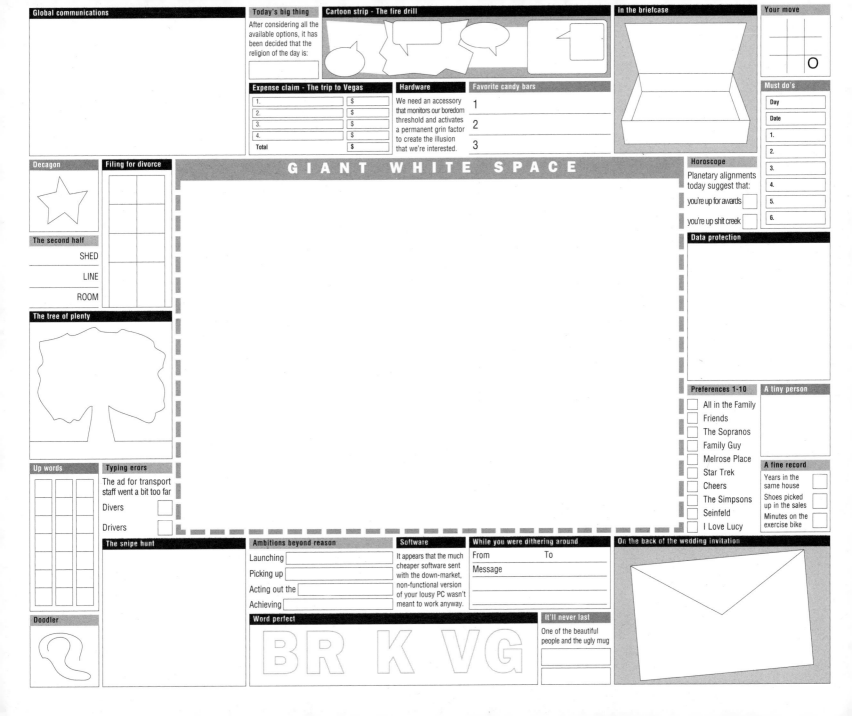

Global communications

Today's big thing
After considering all the available options, it has been decided that the religion of the day is:

Cartoon strip - The fire drill

In the briefcase

Your move

Expense claim - The trip to Vegas
1. $
2. $
3. $
4. $
Total $

Hardware
We need an accessory that monitors our boredom threshold and activates a permanent grin factor to create the illusion that we're interested.

Favorite candy bars
1
2
3

Must do's
Day
Date
1.
2.
3.
4.
5.
6.

Decagon

Filing for divorce

The second half
SHED
LINE
ROOM

Horoscope
Planetary alignments today suggest that:
you're up for awards
you're up shit creek

GIANT WHITE SPACE

Data protection

The tree of plenty

Preferences 1-10
All in the Family
Friends
The Sopranos
Family Guy
Melrose Place
Star Trek
Cheers
The Simpsons
Seinfeld
I Love Lucy

A tiny person

A fine record
Years in the same house
Shoes picked up in the sales
Minutes on the exercise bike

Up words

Typing erors
The ad for transport staff went a bit too far
Divers
Drivers

The snipe hunt

Ambitions beyond reason
Launching
Picking up
Acting out the
Achieving

Software
It appears that the much cheaper software sent with the down-market, non-functional version of your lousy PC wasn't meant to work anyway.

While you were dithering around
From   To
Message

On the back of the wedding invitation

Doodler

Word perfect
BR K VG

It'll never last
One of the beautiful people and the ugly mug

Facial expressions - Relief

Favorite pastimes

1

2

3

Bored meeting

Nobody really understood what was going on during his presentation when the marketing director said:

Acrid acronyms

BYG

MMM

LLP

SAH

Hyperinflation

Covert operations

Place names - The perfect place to retire to

The new recruit

A new post to help in any way possible

Superman

Wonderwoman

Chain of command

Triangles

The numbers game

Visible workstations

Flies on the wall

The best even number

Twister

Good practice

To increase life efficiency, exercise in the workplace by walking in an extreme crouched position and carry extremely heavy items above your head.

DRAWING ROOM

The complete picture

Exploded view

The meaning of life

Checked   Signed

Four dots

Driven one? Yes No

Chevrolet

Volkswagen

Ford

Mitsubishi

GMC

Mercedes

Dodge

Audi

Toyota

Hummer

Short of breath

Pen-pushing

Start

Finish

Qualifications

The minimum to be expected for the post

A good sport

Good at sport

How low can you go?

Bad practice

Walking all over everybody else on the way up to the top and expecting to be treated with some sympathy on the way back down again.

Opposites attract

The incredulously fat and the worryingly thin

Wasting time

One moment in time

Time	Date
Who's out	
Who's in	
Who's for coffee	

Waving

How many?

Brothers

Sisters

Cousins

Putting it more bluntly

Inviting staff to an optional training seminar

Suggesting some energy saving practices

Why is it so inevitable that when you come up with and then plan to present a great idea, your boss breezes in and takes all the credit?

Snake Pass

Today's big thing

After considering all the available options, it has been decided that the machine of the day is:

Score out of 10

Irritated

Cheerful

Angry

Content

Sad

Happy

Manic

Ecstatic

Miserable

Relaxed

Extreme encounters

V

V

V

V

Webbing

Special delivery

Menacing voicemail

Message..........................

....

....

....

Word play

N K

Apples and oranges

Animals that don't get along in cartoons

Lunch on the go

Angry texting

Captured on reality TV

Hiring and firing

The smooth operator with the silky tongue

Hire

Fire

FREESTYLE DOODLING AREA

The Cotton Belt

Small change

Things kept under the table

1

2

3

Interest rates

How interesting?

Mon Tues Wed Thurs Fri Sat Sun

Brainstorming

Best way to motivate the demotivated

Encourage them

Shout at them

Karma

Yesterday

Today

Tomorrow

Flying high

Shapely shapes

Ten pin bowling

Descriptive descriptions

(*n*) Fundamentalist wing of the politically correct

(*adj*) Color of eyes after working far too late

(*v*) Pretending to help with the office garbage

Awful award

Presented to

for their

Signed

A deep depression

Running order 1-3

Running the NY Marathon

Running into a bit of a problem

Running up huge debts

Answer

Rather than a robust appraisal and award scheme, we are going to determine this year's pay awards using a new random number generator.

Low rider

Palatial surroundings

Meeting

During the next dull departmental meeting, try to get a Mexican wave going. Enlisting help will improve the chances of success.

Here, there, and everywhere

Careless talk

Market research

Best place to keep any spare cash

The bank ☐

Under the bed ☐

Big and beautiful

Top three excuses

I didn't think it was important ☐

I was in rehab at the time ☐

I've never done anything like that ☐

Through the blinds

Useless notes about getting dressed

Remember to

THE BIG PICTURE

Office gossip

For today, the person who will not be told what everybody else is laughing at will be:

North/South N S

Bound ☐ ☐
Pole ☐ ☐
Carolina ☐ ☐
Wind ☐ ☐
Lights ☐ ☐
Side ☐ ☐
Dakota ☐ ☐
Beach ☐ ☐
Sea ☐ ☐
America ☐ ☐

Office sports

☐ Put the square thing in the round hole

Learning curves

An odd insect

Lists of six

Things that should be avoided at all costs

Target area

Made for each other

The male and female who look the same

Supermarket bulletin board

Parasites

1

2

3

Blocked off

Error messages

This disk has been ___

Return to ___

Ask advice from ___

Insert ___

Office rhymes

Rigid

Memo

Report

Global warming

Caught in the act

Having extra-marital relations in work time

Afternoons off ☐

No one noticed ☐

Messy

Greeting

When hosting an event for all of your major customers, welcome them with an opening ceremony to rival that of the Olympic Games.

Into the desert

The big chill

Shape up

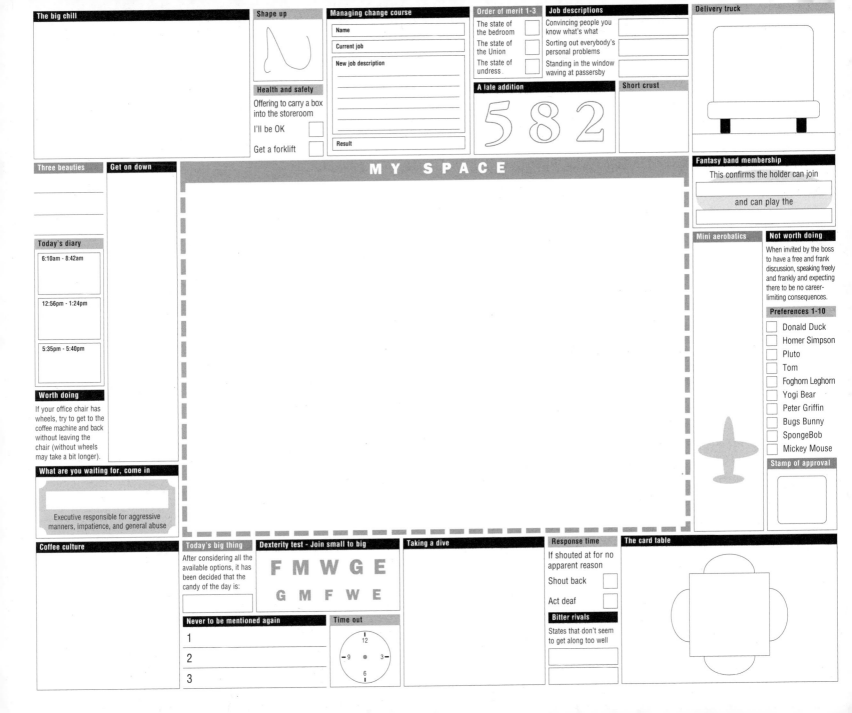

Health and safety

Offering to carry a box
into the storeroom

I'll be OK

Get a forklift

Managing change course

Name

Current job

New job description

Result

Order of merit 1-3

The state of
the bedroom

The state of
the Union

The state of
undress

A late addition

582

Job descriptions

Convincing people you
know what's what

Sorting out everybody's
personal problems

Standing in the window
waving at passersby

Short crust

Delivery truck

Three beauties

Get on down

Today's diary

6:10am - 8:42am

12:56pm - 1:24pm

5:35pm - 5:40pm

Worth doing

If your office chair has
wheels, try to get to the
coffee machine and back
without leaving the
chair (without wheels
may take a bit longer).

What are you waiting for, come in

Executive responsible for aggressive
manners, impatience, and general abuse

M Y   S P A C E

Fantasy band membership

This confirms the holder can join

and can play the

Mini aerobatics

Not worth doing

When invited by the boss
to have a free and frank
discussion, speaking freely
and frankly and expecting
there to be no career-
limiting consequences.

Preferences 1-10

Donald Duck

Homer Simpson

Pluto

Tom

Foghorn Leghorn

Yogi Bear

Peter Griffin

Bugs Bunny

SpongeBob

Mickey Mouse

Stamp of approval

Coffee culture

Today's big thing

After considering all the
available options, it has
been decided that the
candy of the day is:

Dexterity test - Join small to big

F M W G E

G M F W E

Never to be mentioned again

1

2

3

Time out

12

9   3

6

Taking a dive

Response time

If shouted at for no
apparent reason

Shout back

Act deaf

Bitter rivals

States that don't seem
to get along too well

The card table

Your move

X

On the agenda

| Day |
| Date |
| 1. |
| 2. |
| 3. |
| 4. |
| 5. |
| 6. |

Matter of opinion

Bonding sessions are a really good idea

Come here

Go away

Cityscape

It's so small

High or low   H   L

Speed
Water
Spirits
Plains
Heels
Density
Class
Roller
Life
Priority

Best results 1-3

Having a large second helping

Having a pat on the back

Having Miss/Mr. Mississippi

SWOT analysis

Subject - Last month	Date
Strengths	Weaknesses
Opportunities	Threats

Through the mists of time

Take the long way around

In

Out

Strangers in the night

1

2

3

Attitude

I don't care if you've just come out of Harvard, if I say that black is white then black is indeed, until I say otherwise, white.

VIP pass

| Name |
| Date |
| Event |
| Time in |
| Time out |

THE ART OF DOODLING

While you were flirting

From   To

Message

A perfect match

Two fillings for the lunchtime bagel

Disjointed consonants

P M G K L

Platitude

Well, I did say that you shouldn't sit in the Comedy Club front row, though I think he was harsh on your hair, face, clothes, and partner.

Company objectives

To give [   ] to the world

Building a [   ] for the next generation

Making sure [   ]

Being [   ] to the less well off

Name and shame

For always managing to get into work just those few irritating minutes after everyone else...

An epic image

Closed door

Triangle

The first half

SECOND

WET

FLAT

Spots before the eyes

Market report

If the Dow is on the slide

Sell, sell, sell

Use the swing

Ole Smoky

Down words

Doodler

Darkness draws in

Triangles

Falling balls

Reverse order 3-1

Picking up some tips

Picking up the big award

Picking up a nasty little rash

Eureka

New office appliance patent

Title

Invented by

Working drawings

Signed

Mismatched

Deserves total respect and none whatsoever

Vice

It started as an accidental brush in the Xerox room but became a heavy breathing, clothes-tearing, ride 'em cowboy affair behind the potted plants.

Heavy metal

East of Eden

Word association

Actor

Helpless

Pungent

Venomous

Staff vote

Free psychoanalysis during the lunchbreak

You bet

No way

Today's big thing

After considering all the available options, it has been decided that the superstar of the day is:

A full and frank exchange of views - The fax

To

Message

From

Reply

Best vacations

1

2

3

The box room

Door

Window

A box   Chair   Another box   Plant   Me

Things shown half size

A B L A N K C A N V A S

Advice

Get yourself on a TV reality show, behave like an ignorant buffoon, and continue to recycle yourself as the nation's favorite celebrity.

Twister

Figure skating

Possessions

Cowboy boots

Atlas

Sports trophy

Deck of cards

Baseball

Summer home

Tattoo

Poncho

Shaving mirror

Porn DVD

All the angles

Shortcake

Low level flying

Key proposal

Spending the day walking backward

Lack of support

Total support

Pen-pushing

Start

Finish

Cause and effect

Grinning from ear to ear with flushed cheeks

An ability to fall over and not feel anything

How many?

Headaches

Enemies

Watches

Over the hill

Urgent status update

Name

Age   Shirt

Sex   Socks

Date   Contact lens

Shapely shapes

Things to do

1
2
3

Small wonder

Most-horrific-movie-moment screen grab

3 drinks

_ _ _ _ _ _
_ _ _ _ _ _
_ _ _ _ _ _

Cattle rustling

Little jobs

Even if it takes all day, prove to yourself that the eraser will balance on top of the pen, which will itself sit on your computer mouse.

Sweet as candy

Good news or bad news?

Sales

Mon Tues Wed Thurs Fri Sat Sun

New Policies

Picking someone to ridicule every day

Agree ☐

Disagree ☐

The dizzy heights

RANDOM THOUGHTS

Appointments

It is with great pleasure that we announce that the position of the next office loner goes to:

More accurate brand descriptions

Ask our sales team - but they don't listen

The quality leather sofa that's complete bull

The powder that turns all your whites gray

Night or day   N   D

Thurs ☐ ☐
Oh, what a ☐ ☐
Starry starry ☐ ☐
Dooms ☐ ☐
Fever ☐ ☐
Sunny ☐ ☐
Ladies ☐ ☐
Reckoning ☐ ☐
That'll be the ☐ ☐
Seize it ☐ ☐

Down and out

Kids menu

Appetizer

Main Course

Dessert

Marauding mates

☐ V ☐
☐ V ☐
☐ V ☐
☐ V ☐

Shattered window

Time and motion

Irritants to overcome ☐

Taxis until one is actually free ☐

Redials until it's answered ☐

What's the big idea

Whistle-blowing

Using dirty mugs for the visitors' coffee

Acceptable ☐

Not acceptable ☐

Reading the riot act

Dirty words

K V

Libido

Yesterday

Today

Tomorrow

Big jobs

We really need to use less energy, reduce our carbon emissions, and stop the effects of global warming. But car pooling sucks so much!

Twins

Breeds of dog that have unpleasant attitudes

After the tone - The old girlfriend

Message.................................
....
....
....

Little boxes

Quite magnificent

Junk mail

Charity donations to help wealthy people

In tray ☐

Out tray ☐

What do you say?

Divine guidance

Get ahead

To freshen up those boring presentations, combine Powerpoint with a dance routine that finishes with a break-dance climax.

Low and behold

Hidden message

Remember to _____

_____

_____

Happiness search

Enter key elements that will assist your search

[   ]

Results of search [   ]

Achievements

Directives ignored ☐

Colleagues entertained ☐

Pointless e-mails sent ☐

Headlights

WHATEVER!

Lists of six

Parts of the body that should be covered up

[   ]
[   ]
[   ]
[   ]
[   ]
[   ]

Complicated icon

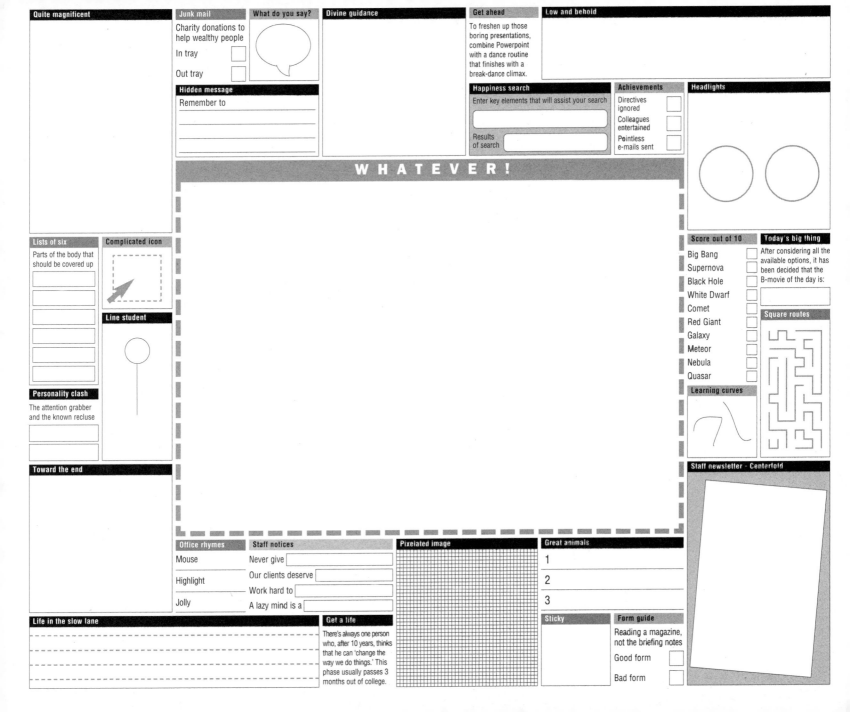

Line student

Personality clash

The attention grabber and the known recluse

[   ]
[   ]

Toward the end

Score out of 10

Big Bang ☐
Supernova ☐
Black Hole ☐
White Dwarf ☐
Comet ☐
Red Giant ☐
Galaxy ☐
Meteor ☐
Nebula ☐
Quasar ☐

Learning curves

Today's big thing

☐ After considering all the available options, it has been decided that the
☐ B-movie of the day is:

Square routes

Staff newsletter - Centerfold

Office rhymes

Mouse

Highlight

Jolly

Staff notices

Never give [   ]

Our clients deserve [   ]

Work hard to [   ]

A lazy mind is a [   ]

Pixelated image

Great animals

1
2
3

Sticky

Form guide

Reading a magazine, not the briefing notes

Good form ☐

Bad form ☐

Life in the slow lane

Get a life

There's always one person who, after 10 years, thinks that he can 'change the way we do things.' This phase usually passes 3 months out of college.

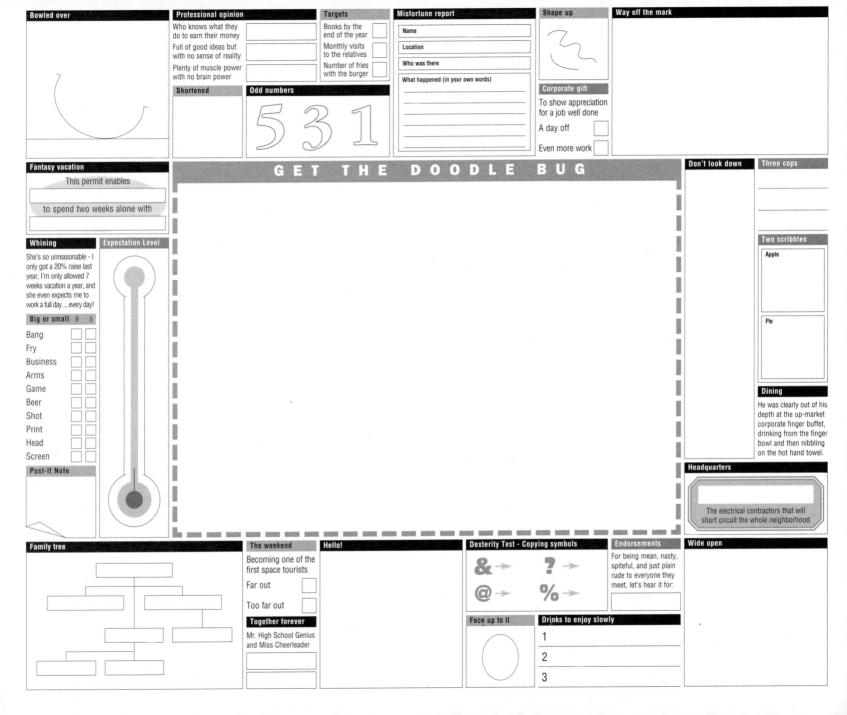

Bowled over

Professional opinion

Who knows what they do to earn their money

Full of good ideas but with no sense of reality

Plenty of muscle power with no brain power

Shortened

Odd numbers

5 3 1

Targets

Books by the end of the year

Monthly visits to the relatives

Number of fries with the burger

Misfortune report

Name

Location

Who was there

What happened (in your own words)

Shape up

Corporate gift

To show appreciation for a job well done

A day off

Even more work

Way off the mark

Fantasy vacation

This permit enables

to spend two weeks alone with

GET THE DOODLE BUG

Whining

She's so unreasonable - I only got a 20% raise last year, I'm only allowed 7 weeks vacation a year, and she even expects me to work a full day ... every day!

Big or small B S

Bang
Fry
Business
Arms
Game
Beer
Shot
Print
Head
Screen

Post-It Note

Expectation Level

Don't look down

Three cops

Two scribbles

Apple

Pie

Dining

He was clearly out of his depth at the up-market corporate finger buffet, drinking from the finger bowl and then nibbling on the hot hand towel.

Headquarters

The electrical contractors that will short circuit the whole neighborhood

Family tree

The weekend

Becoming one of the first space tourists

Far out

Too far out

Together forever

Mr. High School Genius and Miss Cheerleader

Hello!

Dexterity Test - Copying symbols

& →   ? →

@ →   % →

Face up to it

Endorsements

For being mean, nasty, spiteful, and just plain rude to everyone they meet, let's hear it for:

Drinks to enjoy slowly

1

2

3

Wide open

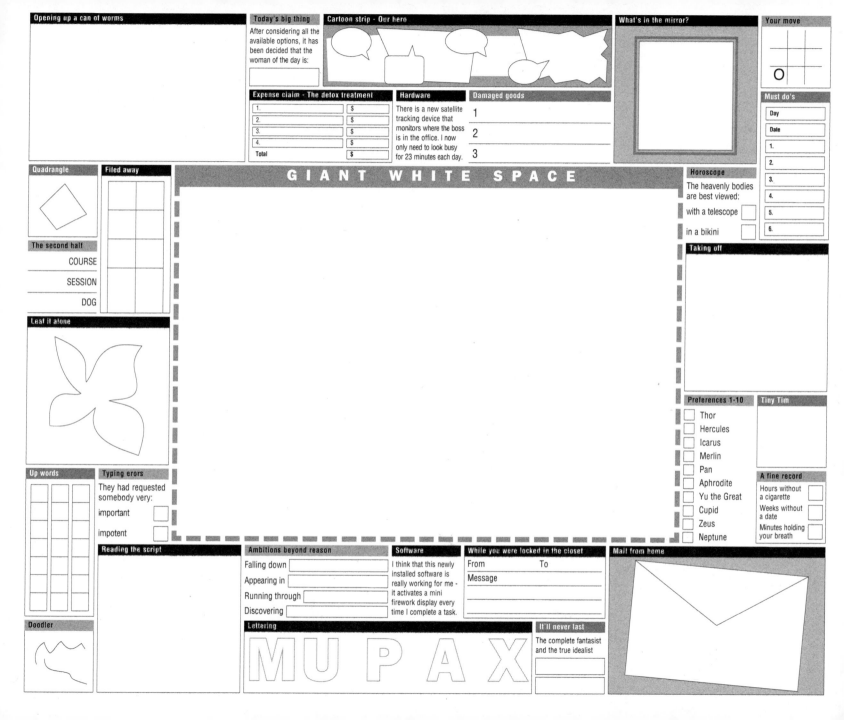

Opening up a can of worms

Today's big thing
After considering all the available options, it has been decided that the woman of the day is:

Cartoon strip - Our hero

What's in the mirror?

Your move
O

Expense claim - The detox treatment
	$
1.	$
2.	$
3.	$
4.	$
Total	$

Hardware
There is a new satellite tracking device that monitors where the boss is in the office. I now only need to look busy for 23 minutes each day.

Damaged goods
1
2
3

Must do's
| Day |
| Date |
| 1. |
| 2. |
| 3. |
| 4. |
| 5. |
| 6. |

Quadrangle

Filed away

GIANT WHITE SPACE

Horoscope
The heavenly bodies are best viewed:

with a telescope

in a bikini

The second half
COURSE
SESSION
DOG

Taking off

Leaf it alone

Preferences 1-10
Thor
Hercules
Icarus
Merlin
Pan
Aphrodite
Yu the Great
Cupid
Zeus
Neptune

Tiny Tim

A fine record
Hours without a cigarette
Weeks without a date
Minutes holding your breath

Up words

Typing erors
They had requested somebody very:
important
impotent

Reading the script

Ambitions beyond reason
Falling down
Appearing in
Running through
Discovering

Software
I think that this newly installed software is really working for me - it activates a mini firework display every time I complete a task.

While you were locked in the closet
From   To
Message

Mail from home

Doodler

Lettering
M U P A X

It'll never last
The complete fantasist and the true idealist

Facial expressions - Horrified

Experts in their field

1

2

3

Bored meeting

It became clear that the meeting could continue no longer when a janitor burst in and screamed:

Acronyms explained

PEB

GHT

LOP

SAD

You're the man!

Keeping a lookout

Place names - The end of the earth

The new recruit

Introducing our new catering assistant

Mr. McDonald

Col. Sanders

Chain of command

Triangles

Twister

Good practice

Visualize yourself as a highly successful person with all the trappings of status, wealth, health, and happiness. Just try not to wake up too soon.

DRAWING ROOM

The numbers game

Pieces of your broken mug

Home or apt. number

Nieces and nephews

The great outdoors

Exploded View

Life after death

Checked   Signed

Four sizes

Like it?

	Yes	No
Running		
Flying		
Reading		
Skiing		
Cycling		
Driving		
Walking		
Skating		
Writing		
Swimming		

Shortage

Pen-pushing

Start

Finish

Qualifications

Must-have experience for astronauts

Flying

Backpacking

Low and getting lower

Bad practice

In the run up to your annual review, embark on an election-style campaign with posters inviting colleagues to vote for your promotion.

Opposites attract

The maverick and one who plays by the book

A scene to remember

One moment in time

Time		Date	
Who's here			
Who's missing			
Who's stupid			

Watching the river flow

How many?

Opportunities

Leftovers

Necklaces

Putting it more bluntly

Requesting volunteers for some overtime

Asking for the waiter to be a little quicker

Why is it that the self-centered, pushy, 'me-me-me' self-publicist seems to get the pick of the jobs above the restrained but popular Mr./Ms. Reliable?

Country roads

How the mighty have fallen

Moody texting

Captured on court drama TV

Small time

Dead people

1

2

3

Shapely shapes

Hiring and firing

Hyperactive sweetie who loves everyone

Hire ☐

Fire ☐

Activity chart

How active?

Mon Tues Wed Thurs Fri Sat Sun

Blast from the past

Today's big thing

After considering all the available options, it has been decided that the salad of the day is:

FREESTYLE DOODLING AREA

Score out of 10

Buddhism ☐
Mysticism ☐
Islam ☐
Voodoo ☐
Sikhism ☐
Christianity ☐
Deism ☐
Shinto ☐
Confucianism ☐
Atheism ☐

Descriptive descriptions

(*n*) Unexplained smears on a computer screen

(*v*) Tidying up after a rather lively party

(*adj*) The peaceful calm before the storm

Horrific honor

Awarded to

_____

for their ability to

_____

_____

Signed

Tall stories

Presidential battles

☐ V ☐
☐ V ☐
☐ V ☐
☐ V ☐

Caught in the web

Running order 1-3

Running out of gas ☐

Running too fast downhill ☐

Running over the neighbor ☐

Word processor

M P

Suitably impressed

Brainstorming

How to really hype up the sales staff

Motivation ☐

Drugs ☐

Temper

Yesterday

Today

Tomorrow

It's a bird, it's a plane

Mail box

☐

Weird voicemail

Message....................
....
....
....

Apples and oranges

The beautiful beauty and the beastly beast

Answer

We have a brand new corporate mission statement that sums up how we feel about our staff: 'Life is unfair ... get over it!'

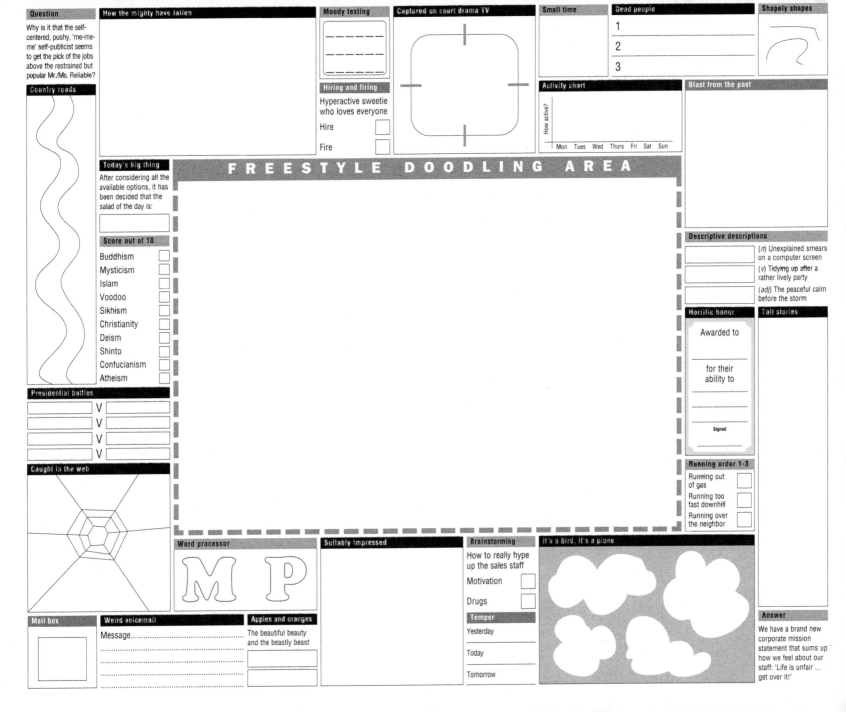

Stretch limo

In the garage

Office gossip

The subject of rumor about their sexuality, private life, and possible lack of hair will be:

Right/Wrong R W

	R	W
Rebel	☐	☐
Immoral	☐	☐
Angle	☐	☐
Normal	☐	☐
Turn	☐	☐
Mistake	☐	☐
Direction	☐	☐
Bent	☐	☐
Hand	☐	☐
Legal	☐	☐

Mini golf

The hole

Avoid the trap

Chip in from here

Learning curves

Police bulletin board

Meeting

Use new phrases to show different sides of yourself, such as 'Thank you for sharing' for empathy and 'No shit, Sherlock' for support.

Top three excuses

Honestly, how was I to know? ☐

I thought she was over it ☐

I didn't know you shouldn't eat it ☐

Close the drapes - quickly!

Rather fruity

Empty talk

Market research

The best place to get really fresh fish

The freezer ☐

The pond ☐

Big bucks

Useless notes about the vacation

Remember to

THE BIG PICTURE

A buzzing insect

Crash test dummy

Lists of six

Really special places to take a lover

Made for each other

Mr. Supercool and Miss Way Below Zero

Touchdown

Trivial things

1

2

3

Caught in the act

Being off sick and being seen shopping

Medicinal trip ☐

New wardrobe ☐

Mold

Blockbuster

Error messages

Too much

You have been viewing

It is not possible to

Please run

Greeting

Make an impression with the new CEO by greeting him like a small boy - ruffle his hair, tell him he's grown, and give him 10 bucks.

Office rhymes

Smart

Chart

Part

Uneven road

Some stars and some stripes

Shape up

W

Health and safety

When reconnecting the electricity

It's all fine

Call Ladder 6

Personal development course

Name

Problem

Participant's desperate need

_____

_____

_____

_____

Result

Order of merit 1-3

A trip to the country

A trip on the sidewalk

A trip into psychodelia

Job descriptions

Eating everybody else's lunch leftovers

Making a major crisis out of nothing

Promoting patently obvious lost causes

Figuratively speaking

690

Shorty

The comfy chair

Three Georges

_____

_____

The long drop

Today's diary

9:14am - 9:15am

10:50am - 1:28pm

6:30pm - 10:30pm

Worth doing

Clear one of your shelves of all its books and files, put down a couple of blankets, and take a nap during that 'just after lunch' period.

Go away, I didn't ask to see you

Director of contradictory behavior and saying the opposite to what was agreed

MY SPACE

Gift voucher

This confirms that the holder can have

_____

for the next

_____

Way up high

Not worth doing

Starting a campaign to make from 9:00am to 10:00am the office happy hour and expecting more than just the office idiot to join in and support it.

Preferences 1-10

Pistol

Knife

Hand grenade

Cannon

Sword

Axe

Whip

Bow and arrow

Rifle

Club

Mark of The Beast

Coming down to the last

Today's big thing

After considering all the available options, it has been decided that the TV show of the day is:

Dexterity test - Grouping evens

2   57   8   3

4   46   5

99   2   77   24

Watching it happen

Response time

How to deal with an indecent proposal

Reject it

Go for it

The pool hall

Things that are just not discussed

1 _____

2 _____

3 _____

Timeless

12
9   3
6

Bitter rivals

Two baseball teams who could never get on

Your move

X

On the agenda

| Day |
| Date |
| 1. |
| 2. |
| 3. |
| 4. |
| 5. |
| 6. |

Get the window cleaner!

Up and down

In

Out

High profile comedians

1

2

3

Attitude

If you come out with any more psychobabble, I'll tell you where you can put the baggage you've made up your mind I'm carrying.

Club pass

| Name |
| Date |
| Club |
| Time in |
| Time out |

Name and shame

The person least likely to laugh at something that everyone else thinks is absolutely hilarious is...

The perfect hostess

Matter of opinion

The best way to get to the top

Promotion ☐

The stairs ☐

THE ART OF DOODLING

Secret door

Octagon

The First Half

FREE

AFTER

BIG

The dragon roars

Microscopic thing

Hot or cold   H   C

Date ☐ ☐
Sweat ☐ ☐
Plate ☐ ☐
Shoulder ☐ ☐
Tub ☐ ☐
War ☐ ☐
Air ☐ ☐
Turkey ☐ ☐
Dog ☐ ☐
Feet ☐ ☐

Best results 1-3

Beating yourself up ☐

Beating your keenest rivals ☐

Beating an egg ☐

Line 'em up

Market report

What to do if the market is in freefall

Get a parachute ☐

Get out of the way ☐

Down words

SWOT analysis

Subject - Best buddy	Date
Strengths	Weaknesses
Opportunities	Threats

While you were hiding under the desk

From   To

Message

A perfect match

The southern belle and the northern hick

Letter's play

OF WA H

Platitude

Well, I did say that if you sat in that draft you'd catch a nasty cold which would lead to pneumonia, paralysis, and a bad toothache.

Company objectives

Allow ☐ after work

Donate ☐ to charity

Buy into ☐

☐ without exploitation

Fish tank

Doodler

Keeping it in the dark

Westside

Word association
Bigot	
Fictional	
Sniff	
Laughable	

Today's big thing
After considering all the available options, it has been decided that the relish of the day is:

Mischief makers
1
2
3

The wine cellar

Door

Wine case   Chair   Wine case   Beer   Me

Things shown half size

Triangles

Planets

Staff vote
Having a compulsory Judy Garland day

All in

All out

A full and frank exchange of views - The text
Send message	Receive message
Send message	Receive message
Send message	Receive message

Reverse order 3-1
Refusing to do the washing up

Refusing on ethical grounds

Refusing another piece of cake

A BLANK CANVAS

Advice
You need to win a few cents on the slot machines, build your winnings up on the blackjack, craps, and poker tables, then stick it all on Red 7.

Twister

Eureka
Robo wife patent
Title

Invented by

Working Drawings

Signed

A great performance

Mismatched
The baddest baddy and the goodest goody

Vice
At first it was just the odd pencil but he was finally caught with a truckload of IT kits, the entire stationery store, and the boss's wife.

Possessions
Widescreen TV

Driving gloves

Outdoor pool

Flowery shirt

Stopwatch

Spare room

Game collection

Paint

Cigarette lighter

Spare keys

All the angles

Short measure

Trick cyclist

Lying low

Key proposal
Having a 'smooch a junior colleague' day

Lack of support

Total support

Pen-pushing
Start

Finish

Cause and effect
Staying silent but with an all-knowing smile

Beating the desk repeatedly and weeping

How many?
False teeth

Daydreams

Visions

Them there hills

Urgent status update
Name	
Age	Suit
Sex	Stripes
Date	Tie

Shapely shapes

Reasons to be cheerful

1
2
3

Cheeky

Worst-TV-moment-in-history screen grab

3 friends

_ _ _ _ _ _ _
_ _ _ _ _ _ _
_ _ _ _ _ _ _

Over and out

Little jobs

Mark out across your desk the times at which the sun hits it. If doing this during winter, use a flashlight to act as the sun (have spare AAs).

Coming together

Down or up?

Excitement

Mon Tues Wed Thurs Fri Sat Sun

New policies

Holding a séance every morning

Agree ☐

Disagree ☐

Mine shaft

RANDOM THOUGHTS

Appointments

It is with great pleasure that we announce that the position of the next Ugly Betty goes to:

Red/black   R   B

Widow ☐ ☐
Hot ☐ ☐
Clubs ☐ ☐
Tape ☐ ☐
Board ☐ ☐
Handed ☐ ☐
Berry ☐ ☐
Alert ☐ ☐
List ☐ ☐
Carpet ☐ ☐

More accurate brand descriptions

The purchasing experience you wish you'd never had

The healthy options that are anything but

Ringtone downloads that will drive you nuts

So high

All you care to eat

Appetizer

Main Course

Dessert

Celebrity skirmishes

⬜ V ⬜
⬜ V ⬜
⬜ V ⬜
⬜ V ⬜

Time and motion

Miles to the gallon ☐

Feet per second ☐

Days before Armageddon ☐

Broken glass

The big impossible idea

Whistle-blowing

Undoing tight pants when at your desk

Acceptable ☐

Not acceptable ☐

Dress sense

Yesterday

Today

Tomorrow

Please, please me

Dirty words

S M

Big jobs

We need to stretch the hand of friendship to all corners and peoples of the earth. It will, of course, have to be a very big hand indeed.

Twins

Always seen in loud clothes with mad hair

After the tone - Your long lost cousin

Message...
....
....
....

Little boxes

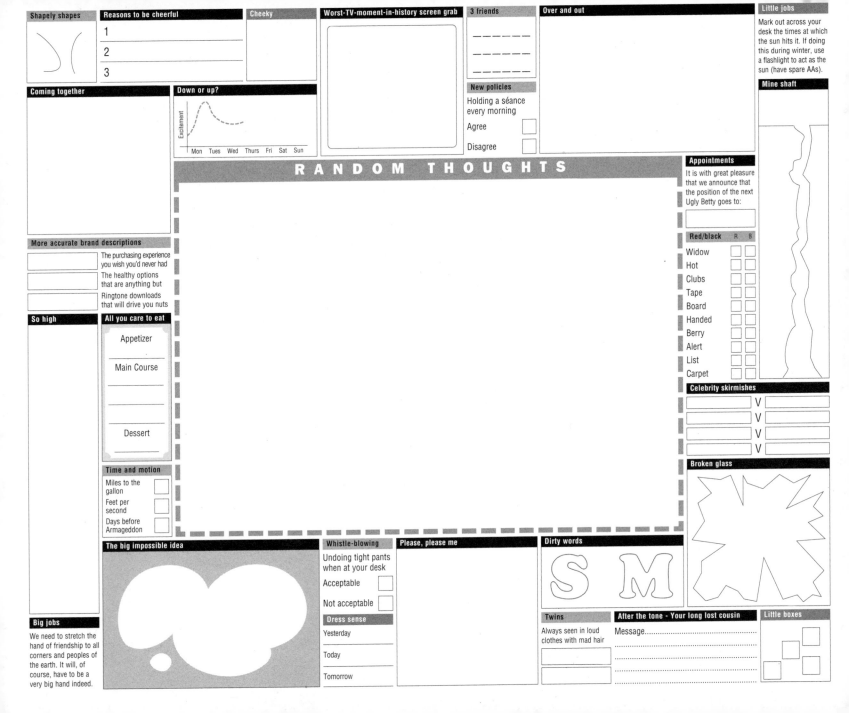

Hung in reception

Junk mail

Offering membership
to the Sick Club

In tray

Out tray

You said it!

Private jet

Get ahead

Be your boss! If they've
reached the top, then
copy them in every way
- dress like them, speak
like them, live in their
house (optional).

Sliding along on your belly

Gotta get a message to you

Remember to

Big thrill search

Enter key elements that will assist your search

Results
of search

Achievements

Cookies eaten
today

Family members
insulted

Websites
visited

Perfect pizza

WHATEVER!

Lists of six

Things that should
really be stopped

Taboo icon

Line coworker

Personality clash

The happy-go-lucky and
the complete psycho

Score out of 10

Florida

Kentucky

Virginia

Oregon

Nevada

Montana

New Jersey

Arkansas

Colorado

Indiana

Learning curves

Today's big thing

After considering all the
available options, it has
been decided that the
book of the day is:

Square routes

Squeal like a pig!

Staff newsletter - A major disaster

Office rhymes

Gross

Numb

Sob

Staff notices

If you need lovin', see

Our customers come

Now wash your

Don't leave

Pixelated image

Fat people

1

2

3

Overtaking maneuver

Get a life

And so you know all
about the policies and
procedures, the policies
covering procedures, and
the procedures about
policies. Fascinating.

Gunk

Form guide

Breaking wind
during a presentation

Good form

Bad form

Potted plant	**Professional opinion**	**Targets**	**Occurrence report**	**Shape up**	**Explain this!**

Potted plant

Professional opinion
Hard to understand how they do what they do
If you've got a problem, who you gonna call?
Guaranteed to get your story in the press

Short and curly

Even numbers
6 2 8

Targets
Sexual fantasies
Trips to the psychotherapist
Drinks before bedtime

Occurrence report
Name
Location
Who was there
What occurred (in your own words)

Shape up
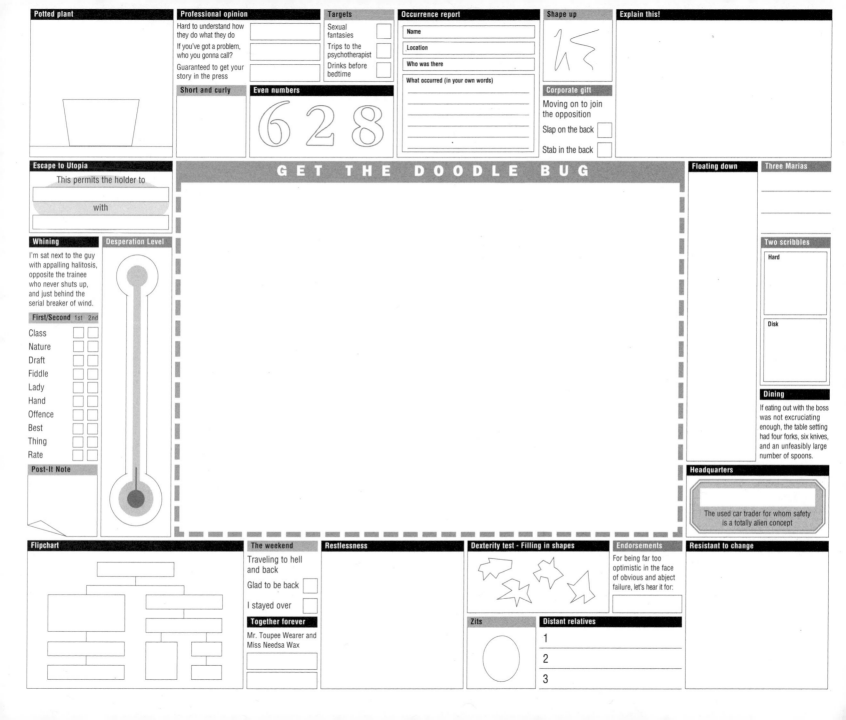

Corporate gift
Moving on to join the opposition
Slap on the back
Stab in the back

Explain this!

Escape to Utopia
This permits the holder to

with

GET THE DOODLE BUG

Floating down

Three Marias

Whining
I'm sat next to the guy with appalling halitosis, opposite the trainee who never shuts up, and just behind the serial breaker of wind.

Desperation Level

First/Second 1st 2nd
Class
Nature
Draft
Fiddle
Lady
Hand
Offence
Best
Thing
Rate

Post-It Note

Two scribbles
Hard

Disk

Dining
If eating out with the boss was not excruciating enough, the table setting had four forks, six knives, and an unfeasibly large number of spoons.

Headquarters
The used car trader for whom safety is a totally alien concept

Flipchart

The weekend
Traveling to hell and back
Glad to be back
I stayed over

Together forever
Mr. Toupee Wearer and Miss Needsa Wax

Restlessness

Dexterity test - Filling in shapes

Zits

Endorsements
For being far too optimistic in the face of obvious and abject failure, let's hear it for:

Distant relatives
1
2
3

Resistant to change

The military parade

Today's big thing
After considering all the available options, it has been decided that the rock star of the day is:

Cartoon strip - The chance encounter

What's in the icebox

Your move
O

Expense claim - Nip and tuck

	$
1.	$
2.	$
3.	$
4.	$
Total	$

Hardware
Who would have thought you could get so much work and personal information into such a small handheld device ... pity I've now lost it!

Favorite people
1
2
3

Must do's

Day
Date
1.
2.
3.
4.
5.
6.

Octagon

Neat and tidy

The Second Half
BAG

LESS

DIVING

In the bushes

GIANT WHITE SPACE

Horoscope
Today is the day to be totally:

positive

negative

Chicken wings

Preferences 1-10
Ruby
Emerald
Gold
Diamond
Sapphire
Silver
Opal
Jade
Garnet
Platinum

Teeny weeny

Up words

Typing erors
The intern had been asked to pass on the:

message

massage

A fine record
Days without an argument

Yards from the fire escape

Air miles without panicking

Spanish eyes

Ambitions beyond reason
Catching a

Wearing too many

Helping to clear the

Tunneling under

Software
The latest virus didn't just wipe all of my recent files, it also seized up my printer, sent my mouse into virtual orbit, and ate my banana.

While you were having a long lunch
From   To

Message

A donation request envelope

Doodler

A pile of letters
Q K M Z A

It'll never last
Same sex couples who are clearly unsuited

Facial expressions - Smug

Classic songs from the movies

1 _____

2 _____

3 _____

Bored meeting

Security had to be called to the conference room after the chairman had yelled at the meeting:

Abbrev.

HBC _____

MUK _____

POB _____

SEZ _____

Icing on the cake

The eyes have it

Place names - The best place to be

The new recruit

Give a warm welcome to your new assistant

Mr. Laurel ☐

Mr. Hardy ☐

Chain of command

Triangles

Twister

Good practice

Increase your efficiency at work by wearing roller-blades when visiting other departments. Build up slowly to a skateboard or small motorized scooter.

The numbers game

Numbers in your phone ☐

Songs in your heart ☐

Uncles and aunts ☐

D R A W I N G   R O O M

Exploded view

The cure for all known diseases

Checked _____   Signed _____

A special day

Four pieces

Scared?   Yes   No

Blair Witch ☐ ☐

The Shining ☐ ☐

Carrie ☐ ☐

The Omen ☐ ☐

Psycho ☐ ☐

Scream ☐ ☐

Alien ☐ ☐

Halloween ☐ ☐

The Exorcist ☐ ☐

The Ring ☐ ☐

Short and sharp

Pen-pushing

Start

Finish

Qualifications

Basic requirements to be a vigilante

Being vigilant ☐

Your own gun ☐

Low flying aircraft

Bad practice

On the corporate golf day, bring your best game, humiliate the boss, do a lap of honor, and use the 'Loser' sign for several weeks afterward.

Opposites attract

A loud booming voice and a whisperer

Boys' toys

One moment in time

Time	Date
Who's not here	
Who's irritating	
Who's wearing red	

Surfin' USA

How many?

Offspring

Coats

Aspirations

Putting it more bluntly

To get the line moving along a little faster

The report could have been more detailed